MEDITATION AND MENTAL PRAYER

MEDITATION AND MENTAL PRAYER

WILFRED L. KNOX

THE ALBAN PRESS: London
MOREHOUSE PUBLISHING: Wilton, Connecticut

First paperback edition

Published 1990 in the United Kingdom by
The Alban Press, an imprint of
Curzon Press Ltd. 7 Caledonian Road, London N1

Published 1990 in the United States of America by
Morehouse Publishing, 78 Danbury Road, Wilton CT 06 897

UK ISBN 0 7007 0225 3
US ISBN 0 8192 1516 3

Printed in Hungary

TO THE
UNDERGRADUATE MEMBERS
OF THE YOUNGER
UNIVERSITY

CONTENTS

INTRODUCTION

In this book I have merely endeavoured to summarize in a convenient form the teaching of the great masters of the spiritual life with regard to those forms of meditation and mental prayer which most Christians can practise whether they are endowed with the mystic temperament or not. My excuse is that there is apparently a certain shortage of simple modern handbooks on the subject in the Anglican Communion. The great spiritual classics tend to deal largely with the more advanced forms of prayer and the contemplative life ; to use them as a guide to personal devotion is as unwise as it would be to start to learn swimming by attempting to swim the Channel. Others are based largely on the assumption that their readers will be living the religious life in the technical sense or are at any rate on the point of being ordained to the sacred ministry ; the layman can hardly read them without being called on to make considerable allowances for the difference of his state of life in such matters as the time he can devote to prayer or such virtues as poverty and obedience. I have not attempted to deal with anything that can be called mysticism in the proper sense, for the simple reason that it can only be described or even understood by those who approach it through their own personal experience.

I hope that there is no advice in this book which cannot be supported by the authority of its proved capacity to produce in those who follow it the Christlike character. It is only on this proved capacity that the authority of the teaching of the Catholic Church can ever claim acceptance. I have assumed that those who use it will be leading the ordinary Catholic sacramental life in the Church of England. If any reader does not accept the general Catholic tradition, he will, I hope, find it easy to omit the few references to that system of devotion. It hardly seems possible that the regular practice of meditation on the life and teaching of Our Lord can fail to benefit any Christian.

WILFRED L. KNOX.

Cambridge

METHODS OF PRAYER IN GENERAL

Vocal and Mental Prayer.

Prayer is normally divided by writers on the subject into two main varieties, vocal and mental. By vocal prayer is meant any kind of prayer which is formulated in words. The words may be spoken aloud or merely framed in the mind ; or we may read them to ourselves from a book or recite them to ourselves from memory, or join in them when recited by others, as in certain parts of public worship. By mental prayer is meant any kind of prayer in which we direct our thoughts to God without necessarily attempting to form them into words or connected sentences.

The distinction is not theoretically a very good one. Prayer can be defined as the lifting up of the soul to God. If this is what prayer is, it follows that there can be no form of prayer which is not mental prayer. For the recitation of words in the ways described is not prayer at all except in so far as the reciting of words is accompanied by a lifting up of the soul to God. And in so far as it is accompanied by a lifting up of the soul to God, it is obviously not merely vocal but also mental prayer.

Nor is the phrase mental prayer entirely free from objection. It might seem in contrast with vocal prayer to imply that if we are to practise it we must not make use of words at all while we are engaged in it. This would for most people be very difficult at the outset. We shall see that in the case of meditation, with which we usually begin the practice of mental prayer, we make use of more or less consecutive trains of reasoning to suggest motives for raising up our souls to God. We shall very probably find it almost impossible at first to carry out this process of reasoning without framing our thoughts into more or less formal sentences. Similarly in the acts of the will in which we lift up our souls to God we shall usually find it of considerable assistance to make use of short phrases, expressing the attitude of our soul to God, as a means of putting ourselves into the attitude in question. For as a rule many people at least do a great deal, if not most, of their thinking in fairly clearly formulated words. This, however, does not mean that such prayer is not mental prayer. The distinction is that the words are merely an expression of our thoughts and our emotional attitudes, not a means for evoking such thoughts or attitudes. Even though at first we cannot dispense with formulated sentences, we shall find later that they will vanish more or less completely. It is indeed quite possible that from the outset we shall be able to dispense with them, though we may go on to the end expressing our attitudes of the soul in single words or brief phrases, such as those described below (p. 80).

There is a further objection to the term mental prayer, since it suggests that it is in the

nature of an intellectual exercise, which demands a high degree of theological ability
and knowledge.   As a matter of fact it demands
nothing of the kind.   The only intellectual
ability required is the power to understand and
appreciate the Christian ideal as it is set before
us in the person of Him who said, " Suffer the
little children to come unto Me."   In other
words, the standard of intellectual ability
required for the practice of mental prayer is
the power to understand the teaching of Our
Lord as given us in the three Synoptic Gospels
and to endeavour to apply it to our daily lives.
In fact, the amount of intellectual ability
required is the amount necessary to save us
from being certified as lunatics.   We shall see
later on that there are various forms of mental
prayer and that some kinds do not suit some
people ; but this is not due to their lack of
intellectual capacity but to their peculiarities
of temperament.   A further objection to the
term mental prayer is that it seems to imply
that mental prayer consists mainly in the work-

ing out of a reasoned train of thought. This is entirely wrong. Prayer is the lifting up of the soul to God ; the use of any form of reasoning in prayer is to provide us with motives for directing our wills and emotions towards God more fully than we have hitherto done. The use of reasoning in mental prayer is a means to this end ; it is not an end in itself, and it has nothing to do with theological speculation of any kind.

Subject to these qualifications the distinction is a convenient one. Vocal prayer covers the ordinary forms of public worship, in which the prayers of the congregation are formulated into words (it does not matter for the present purpose whether they are recited by all those present or only by an officiant, or whether the words are composed *ex tempore* or follow a fixed liturgical form), all prayers which we recite from books or from memory, and all prayers in which we are definitely concerned to formulate our thoughts into words as we go along. Mental prayer consists of all acts of prayer and worship in which the soul is raised to God by the use of formal trains of reasoning or by the activity of the affections and the will : it is irrelevant whether our mind formulates these thoughts into words or not. It must always be borne in mind that vocal prayer is not prayer at all, unless to some extent at least it is accompanied by a raising up of the soul to God.

The Use of Vocal Prayer.

It does not fall within the scope of this book to discuss the necessity of corporate public worship of the kind common to all organized Christian bodies apart from the Society of Friends. It is sufficient to point out that if corporate worship of this type is normally a necessary part of the full Christian life, it must express itself in a form of words which unites those present in the offering of their prayer to God. But apart from this, vocal prayer is normally necessary to the Christian life. We may begin the practice of Christianity in childhood or late in life. To children it seems natural to talk to God in ordinary speech ; nothing is so attractive as the capacity of children to talk to God in the same way as that in which they talk to their father and mother. It would seem to them ridiculous to do otherwise.. And it fairly often happens that people who have real simplicity of heart can go on praying to God either in their own words or in prayers taken from books for all their lives. But most Christians, as they grow up, find that prayer ceases to be a natural and easy thing, and those who turn (or return) to Christianity late in life find prayer a difficult matter. This is only natural. We need the innocence of little children before we can enter into the Kingdom of God, and most of us as we grow older lose that innocence. We can only recover it at the cost of a long and laborious struggle, which may last throughout our lives. Consequently prayer ceases to be a natural activity, and we can only recover the power of praying by laborious efforts.

In attempting this task vocal prayer is nearly always necessary. Except for those who naturally possess some rare gift of contemplation, we cannot raise our souls to God without the use of words. Any difficult art or virtue has to be acquired by practising the actions appropriate to it. Children are trained in the virtue of courtesy by being told to say " Please " or " Thank you." We learn to read or write by laborious attempts to master single letters. It is the same with prayer. We learn to pray by using simple forms of prayer appropriate to our age and state of education.

Unfortunately, many people stop short at this stage. It is by no means uncommon to meet people who say they have abandoned the practice of prayer because they found no value in it ; a number of such people prove on enquiry never to have advanced beyond the use of some simple forms of prayer which they were taught in their childhood. For sentimental reasons they have not liked to change them, and have continued to use them until they realized that their prayers had become a mere farce. They have proceeded to abandon the use of prayer instead of enquiring whether there were not more suitable forms of prayer available.

This difficulty may to some extent be met by the use of more developed forms of vocal prayer. But in the majority of cases the use of vocal prayer alone will not produce the highest spiritual development possible. There are of course many whose state of life allows them too little leisure to admit of more than the saying of a few vocal prayers daily, and there would appear to be some people so constituted that they cannot use any form of mental prayer at all. But it may safely be said that most people can and ought to make a far greater use of mental prayer than they do, and that the quite common tendency to abandon the practice of prayer because it seems to be of no value is largely due to the fact that the whole tradition of mental prayer has been so little known in the Church of England. At best it has been regarded as a special privilege reserved for the more leisured and cultured members of the upper middle classes.

But mental prayer can never entirely replace the use of vocal prayer. Mental prayer by itself is liable to degenerate into vagueness and unreality unless it is used in conjunction with a certain amount of vocal prayer. This element of vocal prayer is provided by the Liturgy of the Church and the Divine Office. Others forms of devotion are provided in various books ; but most people would derive great benefit by relying less on such books and more on mental prayer, and by a more frequent attendance at the Liturgy and by recitation of the Divine Office.

The Necessity of Mental Prayer.

In the strict sense it cannot be said that mental prayer is necessary. It has never been held that the faithful are bound to practise it, except in the case of those who are members of religious orders which enjoin it as part of their rule. And since there would appear to be some people who cannot practise mental prayer and can derive the greatest benefit from vocal prayer alone, it cannot be said that mental prayer is in the strict sense a necessary part of the Christian life. But it may safely be said that most people will fail to achieve anything like the fullest spiritual development of which they are capable without it. And although theologians may draw a distinction between those practices which are binding on all Christians under pain of sin and those which are laudable but not necessary, it is very dangerous for us to be content with anything less than the constant endeavour to attain to the highest standard that our state of life allows. We cannot afford to allow ourselves deliberately to be second-class Christians. It is easy for us to begin by being content with a Laodicean religion and to end by abandoning religion altogether.

In this sense mental prayer is necessary to almost all Christians. The regular use of it will force us to keep before our minds the true nature of the Christian ideal of conduct, as revealed in the person of Our Lord, and the appalling extent to which we fall short of it. It will prevent us from ever supposing that we can substitute the observance of external rules for the attempt to realize in our lives the Spirit of Christ. It will reveal to us to an ever-increasing extent our sins and failures, and supply us continually with fresh incentives for overcoming them. Further, it will add fresh meaning and life to our vocal prayers and our attendance at public worship, and prevent them from becoming formal and lifeless repetitions with no spiritual meaning.

These are benefits which most people cannot obtain in any other way. And although we may urge that there is no rule of the Church which orders us to make use of mental prayer, yet we can hardly hope that we shall have any very good excuse in the sight of God, if we deliberately neglect the means of obtaining them and content ourselves with a lower standard of religion. In this sense it may fairly be urged that mental prayer should be a necessary part of the life of all Christians except those quite exceptional people who seem incapable of mental prayer of any kind, or those whose condition of life really does give them no leisure for any but the briefest prayers. It will be seen below that this lack of leisure cannot be pleaded with real sincerity by any but a very few people, even in the conditions of modern industrial civilization.

In general, therefore, it may be said that though mental prayer is not in the strict sense a duty binding upon Christians, it is normally necessary for all those who are not prepared to be content with offering Our Lord anything less than the fullest devotion of which they are capable. No doubt those for whom it is really impossible receive grace in other ways to compensate for their inability to practise mental prayer ; but we cannot expect to be given exceptional forms of grace while we are de-

Objections to the Use of Mental Prayer.

Before considering the methods of mental prayer, it may be well to consider some of the objections commonly made by those who do not use it.

The first of these is a theoretical one : " How can I be sure that mental prayer is not a form of auto-suggestion, and that the spiritual progress which it produces is not simply due to the fact that by meditating on the character of Jesus I naturally tend to assimilate my character to the ideal I am continually contemplating ? " From the Christian point of view the objection is entirely unimportant. In so far as the psychologist is able to analyse the effect of the use of mental prayer on the human character, he is merely analysing the method by which the grace of God affects the soul ; he is analysing the method by which God works in one sphere of creation, just as the scientist analyses His methods of operation in nature. It has never been urged that there is in the effect of mental prayer anything miraculous or beyond the analysing powers of the human mind. Consequently, although in fact the good effects of mental prayer may be largely explicable in terms of auto-suggestion, this does not in the smallest degree prove that it is not a means of obtaining divine grace.

A second objection which seems on the surface to deserve serious attention is that there is a danger that the practice of mental prayer may lead to a false conception of religion, in which we are selfishly preoccupied with our own personal development in the spiritual life instead of the service of God and our neighbours, and even result in a morbidly introspective and unhealthy frame of mind. The answer to this is that all practice of religion may produce these bad effects if we allow ourselves to forget the main object of religion. The main object of religion is neither the improvement of our own character nor the service of our neighbours. The object of religion is to love and serve and glorify God. We normally cannot achieve this purpose, the end for which we were created, without living a life of love and service of those among whom we live ; and we can only achieve it in so far as we are attempting to lead a life of personal holiness. But we cannot achieve it at all if we allow our religion to degenerate into a vague philanthropic enthusiasm or a mere attempt at self-improvement ; all genuine religion must be directed to God as its sole end. Mental prayer will assist us to keep this object of life before us ; it is by neglecting it that we shall be in danger of substituting the means for the end.

There are further two practical objections which are commonly made. The first is frequently expressed in the form, " I could never practise mental prayer, I'm not clever enough." The answer is that a person who is not clever enough to practise mental prayer is not clever enough to be entrusted with the management of the ordinary affairs of daily life, and ought to be shut up in an asylum or a private home.

It must be admitted that there is a considerable number of people who cannot practise formal meditation of the normal type, which will be described later, and that there are a very few people who cannot apparently practise any kind of mental prayer. But the reason is not that they are not clever enough, but that they are temperamentally unsuited for meditation or for all kinds of mental prayer. A temperament incapable of any kind of mental prayer is very uncommon ; and it can only be ascertained that we are really incapable of it when we have made solid and persevering efforts without any success. To refuse to make the attempt in advance on the ground of lack of intelligence is purely ridiculous. Mental prayer is an entirely different thing from the acquisition of theological learning.

The second is the common one : " I haven't got the time." It may be admitted that in modern conditions of life there are people who really have no time for any but the briefest vocal prayers ; even if they have time, they are normally too exhausted by the day's work for the effort which mental prayer involves. Yet many people do practise it regularly, although their lives are mainly devoted to the most exacting forms of work. And in most cases it is ridiculous to suppose that we cannot really afford a small period of time daily for the practice of so essential a form of prayer. We may not be able to afford half an hour, and yet be quite able to spare a quarter of an hour or ten minutes or five. Moreover, if we can do nothing else we can substitute mental prayer for the saying of morning or evening prayers. We are under no obligation to use set forms of prayer at these times. We can, if we choose, substitute mental prayer for the intercessions which are frequently used by people for whom they mean no more than the mechanical recitation of lists of names, making in advance an initial offering of our mental prayer as an act of intercession for such persons or causes. Unless we are so busy that we cannot find even five minutes in the day to offer to God, we cannot honestly say that we have no time for mental prayer.

Note.—There is of course no reason why we should not combine attendance at the Mass and the receiving of Holy Communion with the practice of mental prayer. We are not bound to follow the words of the service. If we choose to devote the time of the service to mental prayer and to unite our prayers by an act of intention with the worship of the Church and the person of Jesus in the Blessed Sacrament, we are perfectly at liberty to do so, and the practice is a very profitable one. In this way some who are in the habit of hearing Mass frequently and have little time for other prayers may combine their present devotional practice with the use of mental prayer.

The Remote Preparation.

Theologians sometimes emphasize the necessity of what is described as the " remote preparation " for meditation or the practice of mental prayer in general. The " remote preparation " is in fact simply the serious endeavour to lead a Christian life to the best of our ability. We need not be perfect Christians to practise mental prayer with success ; we may even be quite far removed from complete triumph over serious temptations to sin. But we must recognize the necessity of struggling against temptation and advancing in Christian holiness if we are to make any progress in mental prayer. If we are to do so, we must be determined not to be content with any imitation of Christianity. In the initial stages, at any rate (and the initial stages may quite possibly last for the whole of our life), we shall probably be mainly concerned with contemplating the ideal set before us in the person of Jesus, and in the attempt to approach more closely to it ; we certainly shall not make any progress, if we are determined not to allow our religion to cost us any trouble. " If any man will serve Me, let him deny himself and take up his cross and follow Me." There is no possibility of any genuine progress in prayer, unless we are prepared to bear the Cross ; any seeming progress we may make will be a mere illusion. Consequently, if we are to practise mental prayer with any success we must set out with a firm resolution to lead a

II

MEDITATION

The Relation of Meditation to Mental Prayer.

The term " meditation " is commonly but inaccurately employed as if it were equivalent to mental prayer. The confusion of the terms is due to the fact that meditation is normally the first method of mental prayer, from which we can go on to others, while many people never rise beyond the stage of meditation to other forms of mental prayer. But properly meditation is only a particular kind of mental prayer. In consists in the use of consecutive reasoning on the subject of the truths of the Christian religion or the teaching of Our Lord, the object of which is to bring home to us more clearly the goodness of God and our own unworthiness. The effect of this reasoning is to enable us to raise up our souls to God in love, praise, hope and faith, or to submit ourselves to Him in humility, penitence and resignation. Strictly speaking, such acts of the will are the end to which the preceding considerations are the means, and are prayer in the proper sense ; the actual element of meditation or consecutive reasoning is not so much prayer as a means to prayer. At the same time, for most people this element of reflection or consideration will normally form the main part of their prayers for a considerable period of time ; and the whole process of meditation, since it is an act offered to the glory of. God, may appropriately be regarded as an act of prayer. None the less, it is important to recognize from the start that the purely reflective element of meditation is not the whole of mental prayer, and conversely that mental prayer is not essentially a series of consecutive reasonings and that the element of consecutive reasoning may be largely or completely dispensed with. The extent to which this is possible will vary indefinitely in different persons and in the same person at different

28

stages of his spiritual life. Normally, however, most Christians will find that the practice of mental prayer will have to begin with meditation of the type which consists mainly of consecutive reasoning.

The Purpose of Meditation.

In the strict sense the purpose of meditation, as of all prayer, should be the glory of God. This purpose, however, should be not merely the object of all prayer but of the whole life of the Christian. The circumstances of life make it necessary to distinguish between certain times which we devote to prayer and worship and others which we devote to our daily work or our recreation or other activities. But the ideal Christian would refer all these activities alike to the glory of God ; indeed, it might be held that the ideal Christian life would know no distinction between prayer and other activities. Such a view, however, would ignore the fact that Our Lord in His human life is represented on several occasions as devoting Himself to prayer ; from which it may be inferred with safety that the life of the Christian in this world will never rise above the necessity of devoting special times to prayer.

In the case of meditation, our object is not solely to glorify God ; it is not simply an act of worship in the strict sense. It is a form of prayer which ought to have practical reference to the conduct of our lives. At the outset we may still be falling very far short of the Christian ideal by yielding quite frequently to temptations to grave forms of sin. Or we. may be leading lives which are reasonably virtuous according to the accepted worldly standards. But it may safely be assumed that we are not in any way living up to the ideal of Christian perfection as taught by Our Lord in His Incarnate life. The main purpose of meditation is to supply us with motives which will strengthen our resistance to our ordinary temptations and enable us to advance in the direction of Christian perfection. By using it we shall discover how much more

Our Lord asks of His followers than the ordinary man of the world supposes, and how much farther we fall short of the standard He demands than we had realized before.

At the beginning, therefore, meditation will consist mainly in considering the pattern of Our Lord and comparing ourselves with that pattern. We shall always have the practical object of conforming ourselves to His will, in order that we may be better qualified for fulfilling the object of our creation, which is the glory of God. We shall achieve this purpose not by morbid introspection but by the contemplation of the person of Jesus. In the light of His example our defects will stand out so clearly that we shall never need to trouble ourselves with laborious self-analysis. We shall see ourselves in our true colours at once in the light of Him who lighteneth every man that cometh into the world.

At a later stage of our spiritual development we may not have the same need of continual reference to our personal conduct. Some theologians divide the Christian life into three stages : the purgative in which we are mainly concerned with purifying ourselves from our sins and imperfections, the illuminative in which we are being enlightened by a clearer vision of God, and the unitive in which we attain to a stage of contemplation which brings with it immediate personal unity with God. How far this division can be pressed in all cases is perhaps doubtful. But it may be assumed that in almost all cases the stage of purgation will be the initial stage : we may never get very far beyond it.

The Choice of Subject.

The normal Christian cannot simply plunge at will into a contemplation of the goodness and glory of God. At most times he can only raise himself to such a height by contemplating some particular aspect of that goodness and glory as revealed to us in the person of Jesus. For this reason it is usually necessary for us to choose a subject for our meditation.

There are two main ways in which this can be done. One is the use of books of meditations. Of these there are many. Perhaps the best of them is Bishop Challenor's *Book of Meditations for every Day in the Year*. There are many others. There are again books of devotion which are themselves capable of being used as the text for our meditations, although they are not in themselves drawn up as such. The most obvious example of a book of this type is *The Imitation of Christ*, though in using it we must remember that it was primarily drawn up for the use of religious living in community. Many books contain specimen meditations worked out for the beginner, and it may be found helpful to use these, together with the author's other instructions, as a means of introducing ourselves to the practice of meditation ; an example is the *Introduction to the Devout Life* by St. Francis of Sales.

But there is no doubt that the best method of choosing our subject is not to use any books of devotion or meditations, but to go direct to the source from which, if they are of any value, these books are drawn. That source is the life and teaching of Our Lord as recorded in the four Gospels. Canon Streeter compares the Gospel of St. Mark to a photograph, the Gospels of St. Matthew and St. Luke to portraits in which the artist by adding a certain element of his own brings out more clearly all that is implied in the more accurate but mechanical likeness of the photograph. So it may be that the fact that these two later Gospels are coloured by a certain element of Christian experience and reflection renders them more suitable for the choice of subjects of meditation. At any rate, it would seem to be the general experience that they are easier to use for the choice of subjects for meditation. St. Mark demands a greater exercise of the understanding, and it is sometimes necessary to interpret his record by the light of the other Gospels. Since, however, the object of meditation is not to exercise the intellect, there is no point in using St. Mark when the others are available. The Fourth Gospel, on the other hand, presents a different problem. It is the life of Christ as interpreted by the greatest of Christian mystics. It is perhaps for this reason that it has been throughout the ages the food of the mystic, but not very helpful to the beginner in the practice of meditation. At any rate, apart from certain obvious passages, such as the " parables " of the Good Shepherd or the Light of the World, it is doubtful whether the beginner will find it very helpful as an introduction.

Further, it is doubtful whether most people can derive much profit at the outset from meditating on the mysteries of the Birth, Death and Resurrection of Our Lord. These have their place in Christian devotion, notably in the liturgical seasons of the Church and the worship appointed for those seasons. They can also provide us with subjects for meditation when those seasons recur : certain incidents in them have of course an obvious value for us, such as Our Lady's submission to God's will at the Annunciation, or the denial of St. Peter. But on the whole the narratives when they are used for this purpose in books of meditation seem in quite a large number of instances to lack reference to the practical conduct of our lives, or else such references are dragged into the incidents narrated in a rather artificial manner. There seems no reason for wasting our energy on reading into them a devotional meaning which they do not naturally bear. Of course, if we find these subjects of meditation helpful there is no reason why we should not use them ; but it is probable that the beginner, brought up in the modern point of view, will not at the outset find them very profitable.

Thus for the most part we shall probably be wise if we use as the source of material for meditation the life and teaching of Jesus in His public ministry. Our use of these subjects will have the further advantage of counteracting the tendency, which is quite noticeably common in modern Christianity, to regard the person of Our Lord as if He were merely the hero of a " mystery-religion," who has saved us by His Death and Resurrection, and has handed down to us certain means of salvation, but of whom nothing else is known. We must always remember that He is not merely a divine Redeemer, but also a human example ; the modern decline of Bible reading makes us liable to forget this. Our subjects then for meditation will probably be most suited to our needs if they are chosen from the First or the Third Gospel, and if we begin with the temptation of Our Lord or the opening of His public ministry.

At the same time it will sometimes happen that if we work straight through one of these Gospels day by day we shall come from time to time on a passage which seems to us to offer no useful material for our daily meditation. The remedy is a simple one ; it is to pass over such a passage until we come to one that seems more profitable. There is no point in trying to force a meaning into a passage which it does not naturally seem to bear. Later on we may see in it a value which we could not see before. But enough of the Gospels is plain and obvious for all ; we need not worry ourselves, for example, to find the lesson of the incident of the Gadarene swine. In the case of certain miracles, such as those of healing, we may profitably compare our spiritual blindness and deafness, the cowardice which prevents us proclaiming God's praises, or our besetting sins, to the blindness, deafness, dumbness or disease healed by Jesus. But we shall probably not need to go further than this in a search for allegorical interpretations.

The length of the passage which will furnish material for a meditation will vary considerably, and it is impossible to lay down any rule. In general it may be said that the passage should provide us with some clear and definite lesson which can be approached from several points of view. But as we advance in the practice of mental prayer we shall find probably that less of our meditation has to be spent in consecutive reasoning and that a comparatively small amount of reflection is sufficient to elicit acts of the will, which will form the main part of our prayer. Consequently a shorter passage will be needed. Possibly, for example, at the outset we shall find that the beatitudes in the Sermon on the Mount, when taken singly, will hardly furnish material for a meditation of ten minutes ; later one will furnish material for a meditation of half an hour. Generally, however, a parable or miracle will provide us with all the material we need, and some of the longer parables, such as the Good Samaritan or the Prodigal Son, will probably last for two or three meditations. In the discourses of Our Lord the amount we need will vary ; it is always well to read more than we expect to need, and to leave what we have not considered over to the next day rather than to run short of material before we have finished the time we intended to spend in prayer.

Time, Place and Similar Considerations.

Although the mere keeping of rules will never make us Christians, yet most people need to regulate their lives with some strictness, if their religion is ever to amount to anything more than a series of good intentions which never come to fulfilment. If we only practise religion when we happen to feel in the mood for it, we shall probably find that the mood very seldom comes, or that, when it comes, we have other things to do. We must indeed always be on our guard against the delusion that we are good Christians because we have framed a fairly strict rule of life and are keeping it strictly ; this is the worst of all errors, for it is the error of the Pharisee. But unless we frame a rule of life for ourselves (it is usually well to seek the advice of others in doing so) we shall always be in danger of allowing our religion to be forgotten.

These considerations apply to the practice of mental prayer no less than to other parts of the Christian life. We ought to frame a rule as to the amount of time we can give to mental prayer ; and as we have seen, this will normally mean at the start the amount of time we can give to meditation. It is not possible indeed to frame any rule for all people. The general Catholic tradition would normally advise the clergy to give up half an hour a day on at least five days of the week to mental prayer, or to give at least two hours a week to it ; but this assumes that they have begun to practise it regularly for a considerable period during their training. Most people would find it an intolerable strain to attempt as much as this at the beginning. Probably the best plan is to begin by making a rule to spend a comparatively brief time, five or ten minutes, on three or four days a week, in meditation ; our ideal should be to increase this (if the nature of our circumstances permits) to a quarter of an hour on four or five days in the week. If later we find we can prolong this time, so much the better. This system of course is only intended for the layman who

has the ordinary amount of leisure ; if our
position in life allows us a large amount of
leisure, we may very well aim at half an hour
a day, as should those who are preparing for
the sacred ministry. It is of course assumed
that these suggestions do not apply to those
who have peculiar gifts for mental prayer and
contemplation (such people will not be content
with so little), nor to those who after a fair trial
find any sort of mental prayer quite impossible.
But experience shows that the majority of
Christians fall into neither of these classes ;
and although mental prayer has never been as
widely used as is desirable, it has been tried
widely enough to justify the belief that the
experience available is a valid guide to the
capacities of Christians in general, at any rate
of Christians of the Western European type.

As regards other details of time and place,
there is no doubt that, if circumstances allow,
the best method of arranging our time is to
read overnight the passage of the Gospels
(or whatever other book we may be using),

which is to furnish us with material for our meditation, and to make our actual meditation the next morning before we start the work of the day. This has the advantage that our mind appears to some extent to work unconsciously on the subject of our meditation during the night (it is not advisable to try to think about it while we are in bed too seriously ; either we shall fail or we shall keep ourselves awake) so that we come to it the next morning with a clearer understanding of it than if we read it then for the first time ; the advantage of making our meditation before our minds are disturbed by the cares of the day is obvious. If we are hearing Mass, and have time to make our meditation first, so much the better ; it has already been noticed that if we have not time for both we can profitably combine the two. If the morning is impossible probably the early evening is the next best time ; but any time is better than no time.

Probably most people will find it easiest to practise meditation in a church, if circumstances make this possible ; but this is obviously unimportant, if we can secure solitude elsewhere ; and again it is usually best to make our meditation kneeling. It is doubtful whether most people can really concentrate their attention as well when they are walking in a garden or sitting down. But in these matters we are free to do whatever we find most profitable, so long as we remember that the weakness of the flesh will probably suggest to us that the laziest method is really most suited to our individual temperament. It is curious how easy it is for us to assume that the laziest method is that which suits our temperament best in matters of religion.

The Ignatian Method of Meditation.

The simplest method of meditation is that called after St. Ignatius of Loyola ; it is that which is normally adapted to most people. At the same time it must be remembered that the method is rather an analysis of the way in which we shall usually find it easiest and most from our daily life to the work of meditation. It is next desirable to spend a minute or so in reducing our soul to a state of silence, quieting the disturbance which the cares of ordinary life inevitably raise in our mind. From this we proceed to a recollection of the presence of God—we may describe this as a state of positive silence, in which we place ourselves silently before God, the former silence being, so to speak, a negative one in which we simply try to clear our mind from distractions. If we find it helpful, we may recall to our minds some considerations which will help us to realize the presence of God ; we may think of His universal presence as Creator, repeating some text such as a verse or two of Psalm cxxxix, or His presence in us in virtue of our Baptism and Confirmation, or the presence of Jesus in the Tabernacle, if we are making our meditation in a place where the Blessed Sacrament is reserved. From this brief recollection of the presence of God we pass to a recollection of the subject of our meditation. It is recommended by many writers that we should endeavour to frame with our imagination as vivid a picture of the scene of the incident on which we are to meditate as we possibly can. We can imagine ourselves as the sick man being brought to Jesus to be healed, or as hearing Him preach ; we can picture ourselves in the stable at Bethlehem or at the foot of the Cross. But, as all writers recognize, this attempt to form a mental picture may not always be possible. Some people find it hard to frame such a picture with success ; the most that happens when they try is a recollection of a cheap pious oleograph of the Sunday School type, or something equally unhelpful. Again, if we are for instance meditating on the Sermon on the Mount, we shall hardly find it possible to go on for several weeks making a vivid mental picture of Our Lord preaching to a multitude among whom we are seated. At any rate, most people would find that the attempt to do so would become rather monotonous. Yet the Sermon on the Mount is perhaps the best possible source of subjects for meditation in the strict sense.

In any case, it is not necessary to do more than recall to our minds the subject of our meditation, reading it through in the New Testament or glancing briefly at the meditation in a book of meditations, which we have already read before. Of course, if we have not selected our subject before we shall here read it through the first time ; but it would probably be better, if we have not selected our subject before the time of meditation, to read it through just before we start our opening vocal prayer, and to recall it to mind at this point. This preliminary stage of the meditation concludes with a brief vocal prayer for grace to learn in practice the lesson which the subject of our meditation inculcates. It may be observed, in case this preliminary stage seems at first sight somewhat complicated, that all that is necessary is, in the first place, the establishment in our soul of a state of silence in which we are able to contemplate the presence of God in and around us, and a recollection, which should be as vigorous and vivid as possible, of the subject of our meditation. More than this is unnecessary ; if we find that the more elaborately worked out introduction helps us, we shall be well advised to use it ; if we find it unhelpful, we shall be well advised to omit it. Most people will, however, find that at any rate the simpler kind of introduction is necessary if we are to conduct our meditation without being continually distracted by the cares of the world ; and it must be remembered that no cloister walls can be high enough to exclude the cares of the world. As long as we are in the world, its cares are, to a greater or less extent, waiting to distract us.

We now pass from the preliminaries to the meditation proper. We consider first what is the lesson which our subject teaches us, then how it applies to us, and why it is necessary, desirable or right for us to apply it in practice to our own lives. This stage of our meditation will in fact consist of a consideration of the way in which the particular Christian virtue which the subject of our meditation teaches is an essential part of the ideal of the Christian life as manifested by Our Lord, and must therefore be realized in our own lives, if we are to conform to the standard which He asks of His followers, and if we are to achieve the end for which we were created and to render Him the debt of love and gratitude which we owe. From this we proceed to ask how in fact we have in our ordinary lives lived up to the standard which His teaching demands. And here it must be noted that the answer will, if we are honest with ourselves, invariably be the same ; we shall find that we have not lived up to it at all, or at any rate only to an entirely negligible extent. For we are not asking ourselves whether we have lived up to a standard which the world might regard as reasonably adequate—whether, for instance, we fast twice a week and give tithes of all that we possess—but whether in regard to such matters we live in spirit, if we are not called to do so in practice, up to the standard which tells us to sell all that we have and give it to the poor in order that we may follow Jesus. In practice we may not be called to the life of absolute poverty ; but we are all called to absolute poverty of spirit, and it is by this test that we ought to examine ourselves in meditation. From this almost inevitable realization of failure we shall proceed to consider the causes which have hindered us in the past and methods by which we may improve our conduct in future.

In meditations which last for half an hour it is usually advisable though not necessary to divide our subject into three points, considering the same subject from different points of view, but coming to the same conclusion. If, however, at the outset we find that the attempt to do this involves us in artificial attempts to work out interpretations of our subject, we can choose a sufficient amount of subject-matter to allow of three meditations with no absolute unity of subject ; for instance, if we are meditating on the beatitudes we can either consider one from three points of view, or consider three in turn. In any case, at the beginning we shall not be giving up so much as half an hour to meditation, and the division of our subject into points will not be so necessary if our time for meditation is about ten minutes.

At the end of our consideration of each point, or else after we have considered all the three, we come to that part of the meditation which is of the greatest importance. This consists of the lifting up of the soul to God. The effect of the preceding considerations will have been to excite our emotions by bringing vividly before our minds the infinitude both of the love of God and of His demands on us, and the unworthiness of that love which is manifested in our almost complete failure to live up to the standard of Jesus. We now proceed to lift up our soul to Him in penitence for our past failure, hope of future amendment,

of our second point. If, however, we defer
them until we have considered our three points
in turn, we finish our three points and then frame
the acts of the will with which our considerations
end.   We should then proceed to the forming
of a practical resolution.   This should preferably be a simple resolution to be executed in
the course of the day.   It should not be
merely a vague resolution to exercise some
particular virtue, for instance to show greater
humility or to love God better.   It should
take the form of exercising some particular
virtue in the circumstances that are certain
or likely to meet us in our daily life ; we can
resolve not to lose our temper with the peculiarly tiresome person we have to meet at
lunch, not to wade through the divorce-court
proceedings in our newspaper at breakfast,
not to tell anyone of the rather kind or generous
thing we did yesterday.   It is a good thing
to link it on to the subject of our meditation
if we can ; but it is not necessary to spend a
long time thinking of some good resolution

which proceeds naturally from our meditation, or to invent an ingenious chain of argument to link up a particular resolution with our meditation. After all, the Christian character is a whole, and an act of any virtue will react on our whole character ; if we perform an act of love, we shall thereby grow in humility.

On the subject of our resolution it may be well to note that we ought not to be unduly worried if at the end of the day we have failed to keep it. We must not suppose that our failure is a serious sin. Most of us find enough sins to commit without inventing new ones for ourselves. Of course, if we have resolved to avoid a particular temptation, and our failure to keep our resolution has resulted in a serious sin, we must offer our repentance to God ; but our repentance should be repentance for the sin, not for our failure to keep our resolution. If I have resolved not to lose my temper with a tiresome relative, and have in fact lost my temper badly when I met him, I must repent of having lost my temper, not of having failed to keep my resolution.

Further, the resolution should be something easily practicable. We should not on the strength of a single meditation resolve to go and be missionaries in China or join a monastic order. Both are excellent things to do ; but a single meditation is not enough to justify us in concluding that we have a vocation for either of them. The mere fact that we are suddenly filled with an enthusiasm of this kind during a single meditation may mean anything or nothing. It may be the beginning of hearing a divine call to such a life ; or it may be merely a temporary spasm of emotion which has nothing solid behind it. If, indeed, the same idea presents itself to us over a long period of time as the natural result of our meditations, the case is somewhat different, and the probability that it is a divine call is increased. But even so we cannot decide without taking all precautions ; we must consider whether family responsibilities and our personal capacities render it possible and desirable, and consult those who are qualified to advise us, and so on. Meanwhile we can go on from day to day making simple resolutions of the kind already described.

Finally, it is usually recommended that we should close our meditation with a " colloquy," a vocal prayer couched in our own words and addressed to God or to Our Lord, expressing the substance of our acts of the will. At first we shall probably have to make all these acts in the form of a " colloquy," since we shall have to express them in words ; later such a vocal expression will probably be unnecessary ; it may be omitted if it does not prove helpful. We can end with a formal vocal prayer ; and it is also useful to try to collect a text or texts from the Gospels which have stood out prominently from our meditation to keep in our memory throughout the day.

Note.—A difficulty which is peculiar to comparatively recent times is sometimes felt by those who have to combine the beginning of the practice of meditation on the Gospels with the study of them from the point of view of modern scientific criticism. It is sometimes very hard to meditate on the spiritual lessons of a passage, when we have perhaps recently been analysing its compósition, probable source and the like in an entirely different temper. If we begin the practice of meditation and the study of New Testament problems at the same time, as is often the case with those training for the sacred ministry, the difficulty is increased. This difficulty is largely avoided if we begin the practice of meditation earlier. But it cannot be avoided entirely. To some extent, indeed, it may be further met by the use of the advice given below on the subject of distractions in prayer ; obviously the tendency to allow our minds to stray away to purely technical questions of criticism is merely a special form of distraction ; however desirable and necessary such studies may be, they are not prayer, and are out of place when they intrude themselves into our meditations.

A further consideration which may help us is that the character of Jesus in the Gospels reflects the whole impression made by Him on those who saw Him in the flesh. Even if in some particular incident they heightened the effect He made by the addition of some detail, the general accuracy of the portrait is not affected by the fact ; we may safely trust ourselves to the picture of Jesus, our human pattern and our divine Redeemer as preserved by the Church. If in the case of some particular passage we find ourselves so doubtful of its authenticity or original meaning that we cannot meditate on it, we should of course merely regard it as a passage in which at the moment we can find no profitable lesson, and pass on to another.

III

SOME EXAMPLES OF MEDITATION

Some specimens of meditations are given here in case they may be of assistance to those who are unfamiliar with the practice of meditation. It should be observed that they are divided into three points or headings ; it is not necessary to work through all three if the time at our disposal is too brief to allow us to do so. Naturally it is not intended to imply that the subjects given can only be interpreted in the way suggested here.

On the Beatitude, " *Blessed are the pure in heart for they shall see God* " (Matthew v. 8).

It may be noted that purity of heart is not confined to the virtue of purity in its limited sense ; it means freedom from all undue attachment to earthly things ; we should only desire them in so far as they enable us to draw closer to God ; we should forgo them in so far as they separate us from Him.

(1) To see God, which is to know Him and love Him, is the object for which we were created and our only true happiness. Nothing else can give us real satisfaction ; it is merely ordinary human prudence to seek God rather than any worldly happiness which can never bring true or lasting satisfaction. How have I in the past observed this ? Obviously my life is habitually spent in clinging to all sorts of pleasures, which are continually leading me away from God by causing me to neglect my duty to Him and my neighbour, and to give way to anger when I cannot obtain them. The reason for my failure to see God, to be conscious of His presence in my daily life, is my habitual clinging to the gratification of earthly desires, either sinful or liable to lead me into sin. These considerations will naturally suggest acts of contrition for past failures and acts of desire for God : " Whom have I in Heaven but Thee ; and there is

none upon earth that I desire in comparison of Thee?"

(2) It is only by achieving purity of heart that I can attain to that vision of God in which alone, even in this life, I can find true happiness. I must therefore resolve to cut away the ties which bind me to the love of riches, comfort, earthly reputation, sinful pleasures, friends who turn me from Jesus, and all similar obstacles to purity of heart. I have known this all along; yet I have always neglected to take any steps to remove these obstacles which have in the past blinded me. This will suggest acts of humility for our past blindness and of resignation of ourselves to the abandonment of all that stands between us and Jesus.

(3) The blessing promised to the pure in heart will be the only thing worth desiring even in this life; for only the vision of God can afford me true happiness now. But the blessing promised in this life is merely the prelude to the eternal vision of God. It will cost me much to obtain it, but what shall it

profit a man if he shall gain the whole world and lose his own soul ? It is only because I have wasted my time in the past by clinging to pleasures which have not satisfied me that I now find it so hard to contemplate abandoning them. I must resolve to do so without further delay. Here we may make a more careful examination of particular pleasures which separate us from God by leading us frequently into sin, and make acts of contrition for the sins into which they have led us ; to these we may add acts of faith and hope in the willingness of Our Lord to help us to follow Him. Our considerations will probably have suggested to us some suitable resolution for the day.

On the Healing of the Daughter of the Syro-Phœnician Woman (Matthew xv. 21-28).

The vividness with which this incident is described here and in the other synoptic Gospels will make it fairly easy for us to form a mental picture of the scene. Our prayer after this may naturally be for grace to persevere in prayer in spite of difficulties.

(1) Jesus does not at first take any notice of the woman's request. She is a Gentile, not of the house of Israel. In a sense I am worse than she, for I have been brought up in the Church, yet I have not her faith. I must cry out after Jesus from a distance ; my sins prevent me from coming close to Him. Yet I have always behaved as if I had a right to expect an immediate answer to prayer ; I have neglected it when it seemed difficult, and been depressed and discontented. Acts of contrition and humility will naturally suggest themselves.

(2) Yet I need not despair. However little I have deserved to be heard, yet I have only to come to Jesus and He will hear me. If at first He seems not to listen, it is only in order that He may prove my faith and teach me to serve Him for His own sake, not for any consolation that religion may bring. I have been ready to be depressed in the past by my

difficulties ; I must learn to see in them proof of the love of Jesus. " Whom the Lord loveth; he chasteneth." Acts of contrition, love and gratitude will follow, with general resolutions of perseverance in future and resignation to endure any difficulties in prayer which God may send me.

(3) My soul, like the woman's daughter, is " grievously vexed " with my sins and my selfishness. Yet Jesus will not refuse my prayer for its healing. In this part of the meditation we may in imagination lay our souls at the feet of Jesus with all their sins and weaknesses, particularly any besetting sin which we are trying to conquer, casting ourselves on Him with hope and confidence in His power to save us where we have failed. If He seems not to have heard us in the past in our prayers for help to overcome them, it is only because He has wanted to test our power to persevere in faith so that our victory in the end might be more precious : we may before have asked for grace to overcome temptation without

having any genuine desire to abandon our sins.

The Parable of the Lost Sheep (Luke xv. 3-7).

Again if we find it helpful we can frame a mental picture of Jesus, the Good Shepherd, seeking for the sheep that is lost. We shall naturally ask for the grace of deeper repentance.

(1) We can only find our way to Jesus because He came into the world to seek us and seeks us now. We can prevent Him from finding us by refusing to hear His voice when He calls us to repent. Yet in the past we have again and again avoided Him in His search for us by refusing to repent. This will naturally lead to acts of sorrow for our past refusal to turn to Him and of love and gratitude for the further opportunities that He has allowed us by not abandoning His search for us.

(2) We consider the amazing fact that the repentance of a sinner gives joy to Jesus Himself. He is all and we are nothing, yet He loves us so well that we can bring joy to

Him. Yet in the past we have refused to give Him that joy by persevering in sin or at least in indifference. Our feeble pretence of Christianity, however outwardly virtuous we may have been, has never been anything that could cause the angels in Heaven to rejoice. Indeed, it may very well have been worse than the open sins of many whom the world despises. There is more hope for the open sinner than for the Pharisee, and we shall probably find that we have been Pharisees— the ninety and nine self-righteous persons who refuse to see their need of repentance. This will suggest acts of contrition for our luke-warmness, and of humility provoked by the sight of ourselves as we really are.

(3) There are not really such people as the ninety and nine who need no repentance. "All have sinned and come short of the glory of God." Those who do not see their need of repentance simply deceive themselves. We may at this point profitably ask ourselves whether we are refusing to repent of some

obvious sin or merely sinning by selfishness and lukewarmness. In either case we must resolve on a fresh start and a firmer purpose of amendment, particularly in any part of our daily lives in which these failings have been conspicuous. Without such amendment we can never hope that Jesus will find us ; it is these failings that hide us from Him. These considerations will naturally lead to acts of faith, hope and love towards Jesus, and to a resolution to amend our lives in any particular respect in which we have noticeably fallen short. We should resolve on one particular amendment for to-day.

On the saying, " Render unto Cæsar the things that are Cæsar's and unto God the things that are God's " (Matthew xxii. 21).

As before we can make a mental picture of Jesus talking to the Pharisees and Herodians and pointing to Cæsar's head on the tribute-money.

(1) The things we owe to Cæsar are merely

67

concerned with the unimportant side of life, material security, prosperity and the like. We must of course do our duty towards the order and authority of the world ; but all these things are of very small importance. We ought not to need to trouble ourselves with the question whether we are doing our duty in our ordinary worldly relations. Yet we shall probably find that there is much amiss ; that we have not done our duty by those who work for us or those for whom we work ; that we have neglected obvious duties. Yet if we have been unfaithful in the unrighteous Mammon, how can we be entrusted with true riches ? The test of the true Christian is his honesty and generosity towards others in the trivial affairs of daily life. If he has not learned to love his brother, whom he has seen, how shall he love God Whom he has not seen ? We must offer our sorrow for failures in these matters ; possibly this consideration will suggest a resolution for the day.

(2) But to God we owe everything. All

we have is God's, for it comes from Him, and is a trust committed to our charge, for which we shall have one day to render an account. Have we rendered everything to Him, using all our material wealth for His service, consecrating all our natural abilities to Him, and recognizing His complete claim to all our being ? If not, we have failed to render unto God the things that are God's ; for all these things and everything else we can imagine are His. This will suggest further contrition, and resignation of ourselves and all we have to God by a fresh act of self-consecration to Jesus and His service. We may add acts of love to Him for all He has given us. " What reward shall I render unto the Lord for all the benefits He hath done unto me ? "

(3) We may now return to consider the mutual relations of Cæsar and God. After all, Cæsar has his importance, since the world in which we live is the sphere in which we have to show our fidelity to God. Everything we are or have is His ; but it has to be used for

the benefit of those about us. Have I really tried to love my neighbour as myself? Have I considered matters of business or politics merely in the light of my own personal interests? In so far as I have failed I have not merely failed my neighbour but God Himself. Here we may consider again all our relations to our family, our neighbours and society in general; we shall normally find that we have been entirely selfish; and our selfishness has meant preferring ourselves not merely to man but to Jesus, whom we either serve or neglect in the person of His little ones. Here we may make fresh acts of love towards God and towards our neighbours for His sake.

On the saying, " Not every one that saith unto Me, Lord, Lord, shall enter into the Kingdom of Heaven, but he that doeth the will of my Father which is in Heaven " (Matthew vii. 21).

(1) Outward signs of devotion are of no value except in so far as they express our love

of God and enable it to become more real by expressing itself. The keeping of rules of life in matters of this kind or any external marks of piety are a danger if we once allow ourselves to mistake them for the end of religion. True religion is the love of God and of our neighbour. How have I observed this ? We shall probably find, if we are honest with ourselves, that in a great many matters we have allowed the performance of religious duties to be a substitute for religion. We cannot dispense with such things ; we should need to be perfect already, before we could do so ; but we shall find that we quite often allow ourselves to be satisfied with external performances, to the neglect of the weightier matters of the Law.

(2) The only thing that matters in this world is to obey the will of God. By conforming to His will we fulfil the purpose for which we were created. The whole universe obeys His will. Man, the highest of all created things, is the only one which has the power

to choose whether to obey or to disobey. It is that freedom that makes him the highest of all creatures. Yet how often, almost how invariably, do I use that freedom not to obey Him, and so fulfil the destiny for which He created me, but for the opposite purpose? I can only find happiness in fulfilling the purpose of God; yet I am continually seeking for it in disobedience, although experience shows me that I can never find it there. Here we shall naturally be led to sorrow for our past acts of disobedience and of submission to the will of God. " Teach me to do the thing that pleaseth thee, for thou art my God."

(3) To enter into the Kingdom of Heaven does not simply mean to go to Heaven when we die. The Kingdom of Heaven exists in this world. We can enter into it only by establishing it, or rather by allowing God to establish it, within ourselves. We enter by conforming ourselves to the pattern of Jesus in all things. As long as any part of our lives is separated from the love of God and of our

neighbour, we are not fully members of the Kingdom. We are rebels trying to make terms of peace instead of offering that unconditional surrender which Jesus demands. We must renew our self-surrender to the will of God as revealed in Jesus ; this will suggest further acts of submission and self-surrender to the love of God.

Summary of the Ignatian Method.

In case it may prove of value, an analysis of the various stages of the Ignatian type of meditation is appended. It should, however, always be remembered that these stages are not to be regarded as binding rules, and that a rigid adherence to them as a matter of obligation is not to be aimed at.

The " remote preparation " consisting simply of the firm resolve to live a life of Christian holiness.

The " immediate preparation," which consists of the reading through of the subject, if possible overnight.

F

The beginning of the meditation, which comprises :

>Opening vocal prayer.
>
>The establishment of silence in the soul.
>
>Recollection of the presence of God.

Mental picture of the subject of meditation, or a brief recollection of it, and prayer for grace to apply its teaching in practice.

Considerations.

>What does the subject teach ?
>
>How is it to be applied in practice ?
>
>Why is it necessary, right, desirable, or what motives of love, hope and duty lead me to want to achieve it ?
>
>How have I in the past lived up to the teaching of the subject of my meditation ?
>
>How may I in future amend my life so as to live up to it better ?

Acts of faith, hope, love, contrition, humility, resignation, desire for God, etc.

Practical resolution for to-day.

Colloquy, or vocal prayer summarizing the

acts of the will already made, or renewal of those acts.

The essential part of the meditation is of course the comparison of the teaching of the subject of the meditation with my own past attempts to realize that teaching in practice, and the formation of acts of the will intended to make me do so better in future.

Acts of the Will.

Probably most people who have not made any regular practice of meditation will find great difficulty in forming acts of the will, and may even find the phrase hard to understand. It is simplest to explain the nature of such acts by the forms of vocal prayer in which these acts of the will can be expressed. The most familiar forms are probably the acts of faith, hope, love and contrition which are fairly frequently to be met with in books of devotion. They run thus :—

Faith. My God, I believe in Thee and all

Thy Church doth teach, because Thou hast said it and Thy word is true.

Hope. My God, I hope in Thee for grace and for glory, because of Thy promises, Thy mercy and Thy power.

Love. My God, I love Thee with all my heart, because Thou art so good, and for Thy sake I love my neighbour as myself.

Contrition. My God, I am sorry with all my heart that I have sinned against Thee, Who art so good, and by Thy grace I resolve not to sin again.

We are not here concerned with the question of whether these forms are as well expressed as they might be ; they are merely selected as being fairly familiar. Now when we repeat these words one of three things may be happening in our minds. We may in the first place be thinking of something entirely different and merely repeat the words because we are in the custom of using them in our prayers, or because they happen to come in a book we are using. Obviously, if we merely repeat the words thus without any attention, we are not praying ; we are merely using vain repetitions as the heathen do ; we might as well be turning a praying-wheel. Or we may frame the words with our lips because they are familiar to us and because they are a spontaneous accurate expression of a state of mind through which we happen to be passing. Our minds may be lifted up to God in the sentiments which these words express, and the words may come to our lips as a natural expression of our thoughts. In this case, though there is no reason why we should not use the words if we wish, there is obviously no value in the words. The value lies in the fact that our minds are directed to God in this way already ; whether we choose to express our thoughts in words or not is entirely unimportant.

Normally, however, neither of these processes is happening when we recite the words. We are as a rule intending to say our prayers, and trying to do so as devoutly as we can, though at the same time we are probably having to resist a considerable tendency to be distracted and inattentive. The effect of the recitation of the words is to put our minds to a greater or less extent into that attitude towards God which the words express ; and the value of the recitation of the words lies in the extent to which they succeed in producing that attitude in our minds.

Now these and similar attitudes of mind do not depend for their existence on the use of forms of words. They can exist quite apart from such forms. They are, moreover, not limited to the time which it takes to utter the words in question ; we can learn to extend the time for which we can keep our minds in these attitudes towards God without the use of words, just as we could learn to prolong the attitude of mind in question by reciting the words extremely slowly. The object of meditation is to suggest to us lines of thought which will enable us to put ourselves into these and similar dispositions towards God without necessarily using any words at all ; though often we may find it helpful at the beginning to assist our attention by repeating suitable words from the Psalms or from familiar hymns or similar sources during the process. Or we may find it more useful to express our attitude of mind in our own words ; we need not be ashamed to express ourselves in language entirely devoid of literary merit, for the noblest of human language is utterly unworthy of the majesty of God, and the feeblest, if it expresses the devotion of our hearts, is acceptable to Him. It is only in public worship that we must try to make our words as worthy of Him as we can.

Obviously the forms of words quoted above are not an exhaustive list of the attitudes of the soul towards God which can legitimately be produced by our meditations. Nor are they necessarily the best forms for expressing the particular attitudes described ; as has been observed above they are selected as fairly familiar instances. It will perhaps be an assistance to some readers if other forms of these and other acts of the will are suggested here ;

they are mainly taken from the words of the Scriptures, which are always the most profitable sources of devotion.

Adoration. We may express ourselves in the words of St. Thomas, " My Lord and my God " ; we may combine our adoration with an act of humility in the words of St. Peter, " Depart from me, for I am a sinful man, O Lord." Or we may use the language of the heavenly adoration depicted in Isaiah and the Revelation, " Holy, Holy, Holy, Lord God of Hosts."

Contrition. We may find an expression for our sorrow in the words of Psalm li, "Against Thee only have I sinned and done evil in Thy sight," or any other verse, or again in the words of the publican in Our Lord's parable, " God be merciful to me a sinner."

Desire for God. " My soul is athirst for God, yea, even for the living God." " Unto Thee, O Lord, I lift up my soul." " Whom have I in Heaven but Thee, and there is none upon earth that I desire in comparison of Thee."

Faith. " In Thee, O Lord, have I put my trust," " I know in whom I have believed." " Lord, I believe, help thou mine unbelief."

Hope. " Thou, O Lord, art my hope, even from my youth." " Lord, remember me when Thou comest into Thy Kingdom." " I look for the Lord, my soul doth wait for Him."

Humility. " Lord, what is man that thou art mindful of him." " Behold, O Lord, how that I am Thy servant and the son of Thy handmaid." " I am not worthy of the least of these Thy mercies."

Love. " My God and my all." " Lord, Thou knowest all things, Thou knowest that I love Thee." " I count all things but loss for the excellency of the love of Christ Jesus, our Lord."

Resignation. " Thy will be done." " Into Thy hands, O Lord, I commend my spirit." " Give what Thou commandest, and command what Thou willest."

Obviously it is easy to multiply verses and phrases expressing these emotional dispositions and combining several of them in one. It is not easy to classify them under headings, nor does it matter ; and again it is probably possible to think of suitable attitudes not expressed exactly in any of the above phrases. The only point that matters is that we should train ourselves to put ourselves in prayer into these attitudes of soul, and learn to prolong these attitudes from mere ejaculations into sustained periods of prayer. The ordinary Christian, at the outset, will as a rule only be able to put himself into such attitudes of the soul towards God very imperfectly and for comparatively brief periods. But with practice we shall find it fairly easy to introduce such acts of the will into our prayers and to prolong them for several minutes ; our object will always be to increase the element which these acts of the will play in our meditations and to reduce the period spent in consecutive thought or meditation proper.

Incidentally it may be observed that we shall sometimes find it an assistance in producing such acts of the will if in thought we associate ourselves with scenes in the New Testament in which the friends of Our Lord make such acts towards Him. We can, for instance, assist our acts of contrition by imagining ourselves standing with St. Peter outside the judgment hall, and going out with him and weeping bitterly when he met the glance of Jesus, or our gratitude by imagining ourselves returning to give thanks with the leper who was cleansed. This use of the imagination may be found useful by those who find it hard to produce acts of the will at the outset.

Another Method of Meditation.

A method of meditation which may be found useful by those who find the method described above unprofitable, or which may from time to time be employed as a variation to the former, if for a time it proves difficult, is the following. As before, we decide on a suitable book of meditations or a book of the Scriptures, normally one of the Gospels, and work through it day by day. But instead of limiting ourselves to a single passage and endeavouring to draw from it a single lesson, we read continuously, preferably on our knees, until we come to a verse which suggests a train of thought for meditation. On coming to such a passage we meditate on it in the manner described above, endeavouring to draw from it material for acts of the will. When we feel that we have exhausted all the benefit that we can at present derive from this particular verse, we go on reading until we come to another such text and repeat our meditation in the same way. We continue this mixed reading and meditation until the time allotted for our prayer is finished. It will be of some value to read our book of meditations or our Bible overnight, noting texts which seem likely to provide profitable material, though without tying ourselves down to any feeling that we are bound to meditate on them next day. The advantage of this method is that it will enable us to cover a wider range of subjects ; but we shall probably find that it does not allow us to concentrate so closely on any one in particular. For most people the former method is likely to be of far greater value ; this method, however, may prove possible for some who find the other useless, or as an occasional change. We should aim at devoting our time largely to acts of the will, the element of reflective reasoning being superseded by our reading. It will, however, be desirable to be rather strict with ourselves in the examination of our conscience, in order to see clearly how far we fall short of the Christian ideal. Otherwise there is a danger that this form of meditation may degenerate into a rather sleepy and comfortable brooding over favourite texts and ideas. We shall forget that meditation ought to be a means of learning how to bear the Cross.

IV

MENTAL PRAYER

Prayer of Acts of the Will and Affections.

It has already been observed that in the strictest sense the element of prayer in our meditations consists in those acts of the will which the practice of reflection and reasoning enables us to produce. As we advance in the habit of meditation the amount of time we spend in the forming of such acts of the will generally increases ; the amount of time needed for reflection is diminished. Later the element of reflective reasoning should tend to disappear and our prayer will come to consist entirely of acts of the will flowing naturally from a momentary consideration of our subject, and leading on naturally from one to another. Although at first it will be a considerable effort for most people to produce such acts and to persevere in them for any length of time, it offer ourselves and all that we are or have to Him, in order that He may be able to use us as He sees fit. The clause, " Thy Kingdom come," will suggest acts of desire for God, that His Kingdom may be established completely in our hearts and lives ; we must establish the Kingdom of God within us, if we are to establish it anywhere else. " Thy will be done " will provide us with opportunities of resigning ourselves to the will of God both in general and in regard to our particular circumstances, especially those in which we are to live during the present day ; the meek will only inherit " the earth," their eternal country in Heaven, if they learn to find and appropriate it in the present surroundings of their daily lives. So we combine our acts of desire for God and resignation to His will in the words " in earth as it is in Heaven." " Give us this day our daily bread " will suggest acts of faith and hope in Him who cares for the sparrows and the lilies of the field, and will not fail to provide us with our needs for the coming day ;

whether He gives more or less, the meek will be prepared to accept His gifts with equal gratitude. The next clause will furnish material for acts of contrition for our past failures in the virtue of meekness, especially in meekness in enduring the wrongs of others ; the last two clauses will provide fresh occasion for acts of faith and hope that God will deliver us from the only peril that really matters, the peril of falling away from Him through reliance on ourselves instead of on His grace. This type of prayer may prove of assistance to some as a means of passing from ordinary meditation to a prayer composed entirely of acts of the will ; it is of course useless to weary ourselves by trying to force our prayers into this or any other mould, if we do not find it fairly easy to do so after a reasonable trial.

There are indeed occasions when we find it easy to raise our souls to God in affections of this kind. Further, such affections will sometimes take the form of a general sense of communion with God, which we should find it difficult, if not impossible, to describe as love or contrition or hope, or any similar act of the will. It includes in general all these attitudes, but can hardly be described as being any one in particular ; it is simply a contemplation of God or of the person of Our Lord, and a consciousness of communion with Him. Such an attitude of the soul is really proper to a more advanced stage of the spiritual life, when we have passed from the prayer of specific acts or affections of the will to a form of prayer which consists in a general fixing of the soul on God which cannot be analysed into particular affections because it includes them all and yet passes beyond them. But while we shall not normally be able to achieve this kind of prayer for any long period until we have practised the ordinary forms of mental prayer for many years, we can fairly often achieve it for periods of a few minutes, either in our meditations or at other times. If we find ourselves drawn to this kind of prayer, we should by all means follow the im-

general variety just described, are not allowed
to make our prayers degenerate into a mere
emotionalism which has no reference to the
conduct of life. It is possible for us to allow
them to degenerate in this way at times when
we find prayer of this sort easy and congenial ;
and we should therefore make sure that our acts
are not simply vague outpourings of sentiment,
but refer definitely to our own personal lives.
They should therefore include a considerable
element of contrition for our actual sins and
for our failure to live up to the standard of
Our Lord, and of resignation to the Divine Will.
A large number of our sins proceed from our
unwillingness to accept the will of God, as
He manifests it to us through the people
whom He gives us as our neighbours and the
circumstances in which He places us. We
are not indeed bound to accept them as they are,
in the sense that we may not make any attempt
to improve them ; but obviously if we were
perfect Christians we should endeavour to
improve our neighbours without loss of charity

and our circumstances without giving way to discontent. It is therefore desirable in our prayers to resign ourselves frequently to the will of God by resolving to bear our difficulties patiently, and if possible gladly for His sake. For this purpose we ought to resign ourselves not to remote imaginary trials, but to those which are fairly certain to meet us in the immediate future. It is, for instance, easy to bear imaginary losses and bereavements of the most serious kind with patience ; it is often very hard to bear the most trifling inconveniences when they actually happen without losing our temper. Consequently in our acts of resignation, as in the daily resolutions formed in meditation, we should always refer to those inconveniences or annoyances which are more or less certain to meet us during the day ; though we should at the same time be careful not to allow our minds to wander off into a brooding over those annoyances and our irritation at the people who cause them. It will usually be wise to continue the practice of making a resolution for the day at the end of our prayers, when they are of this type, just in the same way as in the practice of meditation.

The Use of the Lord's Prayer.

It has been noted above that both in meditation and in the more advanced forms of mental prayer it is sometimes a considerable assistance to fit our particular subject of meditation into the general scheme of the greatest of all Christian prayers, the *Pater Noster*. A close examination of the meanings of this prayer reveals its amazing width of application ; there is hardly any aspect of Christian life and experience to which it does not refer. The Christian cannot reflect on it without being amazed at its wealth of meaning, though naturally he will not be surprised. Each clause can be made into the material for a separate meditation ; and into the various clauses when taken together we can fit the lessons of almost any subject of meditation taken from the Gospel narratives. A scheme of meditations on the Lord's Prayer

is given here ; and .it is probable that some
people will find that the ideas of these meditations can be combined with the ordinary subjects taken from the Gospels in such a way
that our mental prayer will become a very slow
repetition of the Lord's Prayer. We might,
for instance, take up half an hour reciting it,
interpreting each petition in the light of the
subject of our prayer, or interpreting our
subject in the light of each petition. This will
be equally possible whether our prayer is
mainly formal meditation or mainly composed
of acts and affections of the will. It is of
course possible that some people will not find
this method of any value to them ; in this case
they will not trouble themselves with the attempt to force their prayers into an unnatural
form.

" *Our Father Which art in Heaven.*" If Our
Lord had taught us to say " O God, Who art
in Heaven," we should still think of God as
perfectly wise, holy and powerful. We should
think of Him as the source of all being, by

Whose will the whole universe exists in space and time ; we should still owe Him our homage and adoration. Yet He would be a remote and impersonal Being, Whom we could only reverence and fear.

But Our Lord in all His teaching as well as in this prayer has taught us to think of God as our Father. The meaning of the Fatherhood of God is revealed in the fact that He so loved the world that He gave His only-begotten Son to die for us ; Calvary is the revelation of the love of God which the word Father implies ; its full measure can only be seen in the mutual love of the Father and the Son. In the presence of such a revelation of God fear and reverence are transfigured into adoring love.

This conception of God is not merely more attractive but actually greater than any conception of Him as a remote and impersonal Being of transcendent majesty. An earthly ruler, who thought himself too great to care for the needs and sufferings of his subjects, would not be so great by common consent as one who devoted his whole time and thought to their welfare. Our Lord teaches that not a sparrow falls to the ground without our Father's knowledge, and that the very hairs of our head are all numbered. This is the only conception of God which is great enough for the postulates of modern knowledge; and yet it is a conception which cannot fail to call forth our love as well as our homage.

These considerations provide obvious material for acts of love towards God, humility and contrition for our failure to love Him as we ought, and faith and hope in Him.

"*Hallowed be Thy Name.*" The central thought of the greatest writers of the Old Testament is the holiness of God. In both Testaments the eternal activity of Heaven can only be described as one of adoration of that holiness. "Holy, Holy, Holy, Lord God Almighty, which was and is and is to come. . . . Thou art worthy, O Lord, to receive glory and honour and power, for Thou hast created all things, and for Thy pleasure they are and were created." The contemplation of God's majesty naturally invites us to join in their homage.

But the thought also evokes in us a consciousness of our own unworthiness. Isaiah, when he saw the vision of God, could only cry, " Woe is me, for I am undone, for I am a man of unclean lips, and I dwell among a people of unclean lips, and mine eyes have seen the King, the Lord of Hosts." Who are we that we should dare to offer our homage to God ?

Yet we must learn to do so ; for, although we cannot adequately express the object for which man was created, we can best express it by saying that he was created to praise, adore and serve God. Loving adoration, whether expressed in prayer or in the activities of daily life, is the purpose for which man was created in this world, and a foretaste of that eternal life which passes our understanding.

Here again we have obvious material for acts and affections similar to those suggested by the foregoing meditation. Or we might consider how far we in fact are living up to this supreme end for which we are created, and the various forms of selfishness, which lead us into the sins which come between us and the fulfilment of the end of our creation.

" *Thy Kingdom come.*" The whole Church ought to be the Kingdom of God visibly established on earth, and my soul ought to be a centre in which the Kingdom of God is established and extends itself through me to my neighbours. This will never happen unless God is really the King and Lord of all my life. In how many respects do I continually rebel against Him ? I must surrender my whole life and being to Him, so that His Kingdom may indeed be established in me, if I hope to see it established in the world in general. It is no use my talking glibly about setting up the Kingdom of God on earth unless I am establishing it in my own soul also. How far have I really tried to do this ?

But it is equally futile for me to suppose

that my prayer for the setting up of the Kingdom of God on earth will be fulfilled if I regard religion as merely a selfish luxury for my own private enjoyment. " Ye pay tithes of mint and anise and cummin, and have omitted the weightier matters of the Law, judgment, mercy and faith." Do I in fact try to act on the teaching of Jesus in my relations with my neighbour and society as a whole ?

If I would really set up the Kingdom of God on earth I must recognize it in every part of life. I must surrender my will to Jesus, so that He may be King in all my heart and mind and will. But I must also see that my whole life is consecrated to the establishment of His Kingdom in the world around me ; I must learn to love my neighbour as myself.

Here we shall have plenty of opportunities for self-examination, which will lead to acts of contrition and fresh surrender and consecration of ourselves to the service of God.

" *Thy will be done in earth as it is in Heaven.*" The whole Universe is the expression of the will of God. But the rest of the universe, so far as we know, obeys His will mechanically. Man has the supreme privilege and responsibility of freedom to choose whether he will obey the will of God or not. How do I use my freedom?

We may distinguish two forms of obedience. The first may be called passive obedience. We must learn to resign ourselves to enduring with patience all forms of suffering which God sends or permits to come to us. We often wish for opportunities to display signal qualities of Christian heroism, but we can hardly bear a toothache without grumbling and making ourselves a nuisance to our friends. Yet if we are unfaithful in little, we shall hardly be faithful in great things. We must learn to resign ourselves to God's will, by learning to endure suffering without murmuring against God or losing charity with our neighbour. And to endure with patience is only a beginning; the Christian ideal is to welcome suffering as a means of sharing in the Cross of Jesus. (For a fuller consideration of the Christian attitude to suffering, see below, p. 139.)

But we must learn not only passive obedience, but also active obedience to or co-operation with the will of God. So far as we know, God's highest purpose is the salvation of man ; it is mainly through the free submission of the wills of His servants that He accomplishes His purpose. " My meat is to do the will of Him that sent Me and to finish His work." Our wills ought to be so completely united to Our Lord that it is no longer we who work, but He that works through us. Yet in almost everything we do, even in the work we profess to be doing for God's service, much of our labour is wasted because we are trying to please ourselves instead of to serve God. Quite often we say we have no vocation for a particular kind of work, when we really mean that we do not like it, or that we find it too difficult, or that it will not bring us sufficient reputation. We must learn to surrender our own wills in order that we may be instruments of God's will.

The motives for acts of contrition, self-surrender and resignation to God's will here are sufficiently obvious : the motive of love is of course the only motive for obedience.

" *Give us this day our daily bread.*" Only now do we come to a direct prayer for our temporal necessities. And it is only a prayer for bare necessities, and only for the necessities of to-day or to-morrow ; and even so it is only partly a prayer for temporal necessities, since Christian thought has always regarded this clause as applying also to the grace we need for daily life, to the Sacrament of the Altar and to other spiritual gifts. And it is a prayer for " us," for all mankind, not merely for myself. There could be no more striking criticism of much that passes as prayer among Christians.

If we had faith in Him who feeds the fowls of the air and clothes the lilies of the field, we should be freed from all the worries about worldly things, the cares and pleasures and deceitful riches of the world, which so often turn us from God. If we possess riches, we must learn to regard them as indifferent in themselves, except in so far as they are a stewardship for which we must one day give account, a responsibility of which we would gladly be relieved ; if we do not, we must learn to be content with what God gives us. Even if it be our duty, as it well may be, to labour for better conditions of life for ourselves and our families or our fellow-workers, we must try to learn to work and fight for them without resentment towards God and our neighbour ; we must set our heart upon God, not upon riches ; we cannot serve God and Mammon.

Further, we must learn to be unselfish. Both in our prayers and in our daily life we must recognize that we ought not to be concerned with our own personal welfare, whether in spiritual or in natural matters. We cannot say this clause of the Lord's Prayer rightly while we regard ourselves, as we habitually do, as the centre of the universe. The Christian is primarily concerned with the glory of God, secondarily with the welfare of all men, himself included, but only as one among many.

Here we may examine ourselves carefully as to our habitual sins of selfishness. Almost all our actions are thoroughly selfish as long as we are content to live on the plane of natural virtue. It is only when we try to rise to the supernatural level that we ever see how selfish we are. We can offer to God acts of faith and hope in Him and desire for grace to love Him and our neighbour better.

"*And forgive us our trespasses, as we forgive them that trespass against us.*" The contemplation of the holiness of God can only excite us to a sense of our own sins and lead us to penitence. We can only come to God as sinners seeking to be forgiven. The mercy of God is infinite, in the sense that there is no sin He will not forgive, if we repent, and utterly unmerited, in the sense that we can do nothing to deserve it. But it is not entirely unconditional. We cannot ask to be forgiven our sins, which " are more in number than the hairs of our head," if we refuse to forgive our neighbour. If we come to offer our gift at the altar without first forgiving our neighbour, we have in him an adversary, and in God we shall find not a merciful Father but a judge. The wrongs our neighbour may have done to us are, moreover, nothing as compared with the wrongs we have done to God. His injuries are as five hundred pence ; our debt of sin to God is as five hundred talents.

Forgiveness is the necessary prelude to our life as Christians. We must be forgiven before we can learn to grow in the love of God, and we must go on repenting and obtaining forgiveness whenever we fall into sin. But in itself the obtaining of forgiveness is only the preliminary to learning how to love. Here, again, the same condition holds good. We can only grow in the love of God by growing in the love of our neighbour " If a man love not his brother, whom he hath seen, how shall he love God whom he hath not seen?" The love of our neighbour is the easy preliminary stage in the supreme task of learning to love God. And our brethren and neighbours include not merely friends whom we have chosen because we have a natural liking for them, but all the difficult and tiresome people whom God sends to us as our neighbours. No doubt the man who fell among thieves on the road from Jerusalem to Jericho had all the Jewish hatred for Samaritans ; but it was the good Samaritan who proved his neighbour.

The opening for acts of love of God and of our neighbour for His sake and for acts of contrition, do not need pointing out.

"And lead us not into temptation." The word temptation means equally temptation to sin, and trial in the sense of affliction. For the Christian a trial or affliction of any kind is a kind of temptation : it tempts him to murmur against God or to give way to anger. And a temptation is a trial or affliction. Sometimes we do not feel a temptation to sin to be an

affliction because of our liking for the sin to which we are tempted. But we ought to regard any temptation to sin as a painful and distressing affliction ; we should do so if we hated sin as we ought to. Our Lord's temptation in the desert must have been one of His severest sufferings.

Yet we cannot grow in Christian holiness without temptation and suffering. Without them the Christian character cannot be established and made perfect. But we must never presume on our own strength by putting ourselves into positions where we are likely to be tempted ; we must recognize that it is only by God's grace that we can overcome temptation. God is just, who will not tempt us above that we are able, but will with the temptation send also a way to escape that we may be able to bear it. This will apply to temptations He sends or allows to come to us ; we have no right to claim that it should apply to temptations of our own seeking. Often we fall into grave sin by dallying with temptation instead of avoiding occasions of sin. Or we seek positions of influence out of ambition, instead of allowing God to put us where He chooses. We have no right to God's grace in difficulties we have brought on ourselves.

Further, we must recognize that in all temptations we cannot trust in ourselves; it is only the grace of God that has enabled us to make any progress in resisting sin and achieving holiness that we may have made. We must humble ourselves completely before God, recognizing that of ourselves we can do nothing that is good; nor can we of ourselves avoid anything that is evil. Yet we spend a long time in self-complacency and self-congratulation. We must see ourselves to be indeed nothing, if we would ever hope to be anything in the sight of God.

We are naturally led to acts of humility and repentance, and trust in the grace of God, and to thanksgiving for all the mercy which has enabled us to do anything good we have done or to resist any temptation that may have befallen us.

"*But deliver us from evil.*" The word evil means "the evil one" or "the evil thing," evil in general. "The whole world lieth in the evil one" and our business in life is just the choice between good and evil ; on our choice between the two in particular details depends our eternal destiny. But the right choice is not one we can make ourselves ; we can only choose right by the grace of God, and we must go through life in constant vigilance, lest we forfeit that grace by indifference or sloth in small matters which may end in a complete falling away.

So it is on each action of our daily lives that our whole choice depends. We may profitably examine ourselves as to our care about the ordinary activities of our daily life, and the extent to which we endeavour to perform them to the glory of God. Our aim should be to refer them to a continually increasing extent to Him ; no action need really be regarded as indifferent to God.

By seeking for grace in the ordinary details of life we shall be growing in the grace which will enable us to persevere to the end without danger of falling away. So we shall lessen the power of the evil of the world, not only over ourselves, but over our neighbours. The grace which enables us to live our ordinary lives to the glory of God and in the love of Him is the surest way of bringing others to Him. And it is the surest means of enabling ourselves to understand the will of God aright in great matters such as our vocation in life ; if we continually seek to serve Jesus in ordinary things, we shall not fail Him if He has some great demand to make on us.

We shall naturally make acts of faith in the grace of God, which alone can save us from evil, and acts of self-consecration to His service.

Note. It is of course obvious that there are many other ways in which we may frame meditations on the Lord's Prayer, or weave it into our meditations and mental prayer. The considerations put forward above are only intended as suggestions which some readers may find helpful.

Progress in Mental Prayer.

It must not be supposed that our development in the practice of mental prayer will generally represent a steady and uniform progress. The ease or difficulty with which we are able to pass from meditation to acts of the will must be expected to vary from day to day. We may often have to go back to the use of a greater amount of purely reflective meditation, after having made a certain amount of progress in the way of dispensing with it. Such fluctuations are due to various causes. Occasionally they may be due to failure on our part to make the effort which God is asking of us in the attempt to attain to Christian holiness. Frequently, however, they are due to quite different causes, such as ill-health or weariness. As long as we are not conscious of any deliberate refusal to obey the will of God in serious matters, we must never allow ourselves to be depressed by apparent failure to make progress or even by apparent falling back. Although our progress in the practice of prayer is liable to fluctuations, it will, if we persevere in it, represent a general advance when viewed as a whole. The same is true of almost any art we may attempt to acquire. If we persevere, we shall advance steadily (unless we are totally incapable of acquiring the art in question), although at certain moments we may seem to be worse at it than we were a few months ago.

It may happen in the practice of meditation that during our reflection we feel a sudden invitation to abandon consecutive and coherent thought and to allow ourselves to be drawn into acts of the will or to silent communion of the kind described above, although such invitations may have no very obvious connection with the subject of our meditation. Such impulses should always be followed. The object of our reasoning is to enable us to raise up our souls to God : if He draws them up to Himself without demanding the effort of reasoning from us, we ought to follow His invitation with gratitude to Him for allowing us to attain our end without the labour which is normally needed. It does not matter whether the acts of the will have any apparent connection with our subject ; we are not to regard our liberty as fettered to a particular subject of consideration, for the choice of a subject is only intended to help us to concentrate our minds and wills on God by considering one particular aspect of His revelation of Himself in Jesus. If we find ourselves drawn into such acts of the will before we have begun to consider our subject, and if we continue in them throughout our time for prayer without considering our subject at all, we can always allow our consideration of it to stand over till our next meditation.

There are, moreover, some people who find it almost impossible to practise formal meditation and comparatively easy to devote their time of prayer to forming acts of the will, based on a merely momentary consideration of some saying of Our Lord or some text of the Scriptures or a saying of one of the Saints. Such people need never trouble themselves with laborious efforts to acquire the practice of meditation, since they are able without it to attain to the object of reflective meditation. They are fortunate in having temperaments which make it comparatively easy for them to pray. This does not mean that they are better Christians. In the sight of God the best Christian living may be some notorious sinner striving desperately to overcome temptations to the vilest kinds of sin ; we have no means of judging. It merely means that they are peculiarly gifted with the capacity for prayer, and that consequently more will be required of them than of those who have smaller opportunities. But it is entirely unnecessary for them to be worried if they find meditation very difficult and uncongenial, or even totally impossible.

Sensible Devotion.

It may happen that at a comparatively early

stage in our practice of mental prayer we find ourselves thrilled with a quite unwonted enthusiasm for the service of God and with a sensible devotion to the person of Jesus of a kind we have never experienced before. But again after a comparatively brief period we shall relapse ; instead of appearing easy and delightful our prayers will be as difficult as they were before ; perhaps they will even seem duller and harder than they used to. The effect of such an experience will almost inevitably be to depress us. We may very well have supposed that the fervent sense of enthusiasm which we felt was the quintessence of religion, and that when we experienced it we had attained to a remarkable state of holiness. We may further have framed some heroic resolution to devote ourselves to the service of God in some particular way (in the sacred ministry or the religious life or the work of preaching the Gospel to the heathen). In the first flush of enthusiasm nothing seemed too difficult, but in the light of our subsequent disillusionment it is clear that at present at least the task is beyond us.

The mistake we have made lies of course in an error, which is unfortunately rather widely spread, as to the nature of religion. Religion does not consist in emotional thrills any more than it consists in the observance of rules of life or the use of the Sacraments. Religion consists in the attempt to keep the two great commandments ; if we prefer a different way of expressing the same truth, we may say that it consists in the attempt to bring forth the fruits of the Spirit, or to realize in our lives the pattern of Christ. There are plenty of phrases ; the meaning is ultimately the same. In no case does religion consist in thrills of conscious devotion. We are no better for having them, and no worse for lacking them. The experience of such accesses of enthusiasm, which are commonly described as " sensible devotion," is from one point of view a psychological phenomenon, which would seem to be similar in character to the thrill of devotion which a certain type of revivalism aims at producing and describes as conversion. The difference is that in the latter case it is produced by the emotional effect of hymns and rhetoric of a certain type on a large audience, instead of by concentrated thinking on the teaching of Our Lord. In both cases the effect in itself is transient, and there is certain to be a relapse from a level of psychological exaltation to the normal state. In both cases there is a grave danger that this relapse will result in a dis-illusionment which will lead us to suppose that our whole experience of religion is a delu-sion, and we may be tempted to abandon it. The blame lies on ourselves for supposing that religion is a matter of mere fits of emotion.

On the other hand, sensible devotion is of value if we recognize it at its proper worth. It is, quite apart from its psychological explana-tion, a gift of God sent to encourage us to go forward on a road which will often be hard and tedious, and often painful ; these moments of relaxation should encourage us to persevere.

virtue. We may find temptations easier to overcome, or we may find it easier to perform uncongenial tasks of duty or charity. This progress may be actually due to the new delight of sensible devotion, or it may be due to the fact that our more solid use of prayer has really enabled us to make progress in the Christian life. None the less, we may later find that our old difficulties have returned. There is a similar danger that we may grow depressed and disillusioned, and tempted to abandon our use of prayer. The tendency to depression is of course always a temptation to be resisted. In this particular case we must remember that the mere recurrence of temptation does not prove that our apparent progress was unreal ; we are always the worst judges of our own moral progress ; like St. Paul we must be content to say, " I judge not mine own self." To yield to depression proves that we have been relying too much on our own strength instead of on the grace of God. Our difficulties may be due to a relapse on our own part ; it is equally probable that they are merely due to the wearing out of an initial glow of sensible devotion, which was given to encourage us, but has now been withdrawn. That such outbursts of devotion should be withdrawn is necessary ; if our religious life were entirely composed of them, religion would simply consist in doing something naturally pleasant and delightful. If religion simply consisted in this, it would have no more value than eating or drinking the things we naturally like best. In other words, it would have no ethical or spiritual value whatsoever. The joy of religion is a supernatural one ; it can only be obtained at the cost of bearing the Cross. The moments when it seems naturally delightful are of no value in themselves ; they are only valuable if wisely used as moments of refreshment, which enable us to bear more patiently the times of difficulty.

Another common cause of depression is the fact that at first we start practising meditation with the comfortable belief that, as we are no worse than our neighbours, we are tolerably good Christians. As we continue the practice, however, we begin to become conscious of a whole multitude of sins and defects which we did not realize before. We see our own selfishness in its various ramifications in the clear light of the pattern of Jesus, and the discovery is an appalling one for those who have in the past lived in the ordinary state of complacency at their own virtue. The realization of such defects is, however, necessary, since it is the first stage towards overcoming them. The only remedy is to go forward with firm resolution and the knowledge that the grace of God is sufficient to overcome even our selfishness ; we need the faith that will remove mountains and cast them into the sea. There is, however, always a danger that we may fall into the error of supposing that the discovery of these new defects is a sign that we are growing worse, as if the defects had not been there before. This is of course as ludicrous a mistake as it would be to suppose that a hill in front of us on a journey is really growing higher as we come nearer to it ; it looks higher because we see it more clearly. A fuller realization of our defects is a necessary preliminary to overcoming them.

There is, however, a danger that this realization may tempt us into the vice of over-scrupulousness. This consists in supposing that any tendency to sin of any kind which we observe in ourselves is in itself a grave sin which we have actually committed. The danger is one which affects mainly those who have naturally tender consciences, and it rises from an excessive concentration on our own defects in our meditations. We should of course always consider our own imperfections, but we should consider them in the light of the glory of God, not make them the primary object of our meditation. The main symptom of scrupulousness of this kind is a tendency to suppose that the smallest inclination to sin of any kind—for example, a momentary spasm of irritation at some annoyance—is a really serious sin of anger. It may also manifest itself in eccentricity of behaviour, leading to an ostentatious avoidance of innocent things for fear that they might in some way lead us into occasions of sin. In extreme cases, though these are not likely to be found except in those who have advanced beyond the stages of prayer considered in this book, it may produce a definitely morbid state of mind.

The only remedy is absolute obedience to our confessor or to any other person whom we may consult for advice on our prayers. One of the main symptoms of scrupulousness in its extreme form is the belief that we are not being scrupulous, at any rate in such and such a matter. It is only possible to judge correctly in such a case by asking the advice of those who are able to judge better than we are ; and in such matters we are the worst judges possible. The danger, however, is not one to which normally constituted people are likely to be exposed ; for most people it will be enough to remember that natural defects and inclinations to sin are not sins except in so far as we deliberately acquiesce in them. Such acquiescence cannot be serious unless it is prolonged in thought for a quite considerable period of time, or finds expression in words or actions. Temporary uprushes of emotion cannot be prevented, but they are not in themselves sins, and nothing can be less profitable or indeed more harmful than brooding over these symptoms of our inevitable natural defects as if they were deliberate sins. The remedy for such temptations of thought will be considered below.

V

DISTRACTIONS AND THEIR REMEDY

Sinful and Innocent Distractions.

By distractions are meant the various thoughts which present themselves to our minds during our prayers and divert us to worldly considerations. They are by no means confined to mental prayer ; probably most people who have ever tried to say vocal prayers of any kind or are in the habit of attending any form of public worship are familiar with the experience of coming away with a consciousness that they have been doing anything but praying. Indeed one of the minor advantages of mental prayer is that it is found in practice to enable us to concentrate our attention much better during our vocal prayers. On the other hand we must not expect to be immune from distracting thoughts in our mental prayers ; they enter our minds just as easily during meditation as at any other time.

We may divide distractions into two kinds, those which are sinful and those which are in themselves innocent. The distinction does not mean that it is sometimes sinful to be distracted and sometimes not ; it is never sinful to allow distracting thoughts to enter our minds for the simple reason that we cannot prevent them from doing so ; on the other hand, it is presumably sinful if we consciously and deliberately allow our minds to be occupied with worldly thoughts, however innocent, at a time when we ought to be praying. The distinction refers rather to the nature of the thoughts themselves. Some thoughts, for example thoughts of resentment over the real or imaginary injuries inflicted on us by others, are always sinful, to a greater or less degree, when we deliberately entertain them and identify ourselves with them. They are not sinful because we allow them to occupy our minds during our prayers, but because we entertain them at all. On the other hand, there is no sin in allowing our minds to be occupied with memories or anticipations of our work or recreation, unless by entertaining them deliberately we waste time which we are in duty bound to devote to something else. It is presumably sinful to a certain degree if we neglect our work by thinking of our amusements, and so waste time for which we are paid, however innocent our day-dreams may be in themselves. These considerations apply to the time which we ought to devote to our prayers no less than to time we ought to devote to our work.

In the case of sinful distractions it is necessary in the first instance to apply to them the usual remedies against temptations of any kind. A consideration of these remedies falls outside the present subject ; our prayers themselves are of course one of the most important remedies, and we must also, so far as possible, avoid occasions of sin, and find opportunities of practising the opposite virtue. If, for instance, we are continually being tempted to sins of anger we must make opportunities of displaying charity towards people who annoy us, and endeavour to avoid situations which experience shows to be likely to lead us into anger. We cannot consider these questions in detail here ; we have only to consider the methods necessary for banishing such thoughts from our minds at times which we ought to be devoting to prayer. It is of course part of the " remote preparation " that we should be making constant efforts to overcome our sins in every possible way. It may be added that the suggestions made above as to the method of choosing our subject so as to allow it to work unconsciously in our minds during the night, and the choice of time and place for our meditation, are intended to act to some extent as a safeguard against distractions of all kinds, whether sinful or innocent.

Remedies for Distraction.

In spite of all such precautions, however, we cannot hope to be delivered from the temptation to allow our thoughts to wander from our prayers to other subjects. To a large extent the remedies against this danger are the same, whether the other subjects are evil or innocent in themselves. The first remedy is of course to pray directly against the tendency to distractions ; this we can suitably do either in our ordinary vocal prayers or in those which we repeat at the beginning of our meditation. The second is to remember that we cannot normally prevent a train of thought from intruding itself into our minds by direct resistance. The moment we concentrate our energies on not thinking about a particular thing, we begin necessarily and inevitably to think about it. To try not to think about a given thing is to think about it in a certain way. The greater the grasp of the particular thing on our minds, the more surely will our efforts not to think about it result in our thinking about it all the more. In some cases, indeed, the method of direct resistance will succeed, simply because the distraction that has entered our minds was some wandering thought which really had no great appeal to us ;

the greater its appeal, the more certain the effort is to fail. It may be noted in passing that the same is true of all temptations of thought ; it is particularly to be borne in mind if we are troubled with thoughts which are contrary to the virtue of purity, but it is safest to apply it to all other temptations of thought. Direct resistance is of little value against any temptation of thought which has a strong appeal to us. It may be added that direct prayer to be delivered from such a temptation, apart from a brief vocal prayer for deliverance, is to be regarded as a form of direct resistance. We should utter some brief prayer for help, but not try to resist by continued prayer for help in resisting this particular temptation ; for by praying about it we shall be thinking about it.

In the case of thoughts which enter our minds during our ordinary occupations the best remedy is to provide a substitute for them by turning to some occupation which will employ and interest us sufficiently to exclude them.

We cannot do this in the case of our prayers, unless we are going to abandon them entirely ; it is sometimes indeed desirable, if we find ourselves very much occupied with some particular train of thought, to postpone our prayers till some other time of the day when we may hope that our minds will be calmer ; but it will often happen that we cannot postpone them without abandoning them altogether. We must therefore be prepared normally to meet distractions in other ways. The first and most important is to provide ourselves with a variety of memories of incidents (they will usually be most valuable if chosen from the Gospels) which will concentrate our thoughts on the person of Our Lord, and bring Him vividly before us as our deliverer. We can, for instance, imagine ourselves with St. Peter trying to walk to Jesus on the waters, or with the disciples in the boat on the point of sinking in the storm, and call in spirit, " Save, Lord, we perish." Or we can imagine ourselves with the three disciples in the garden of

Gethsemane, and hear the voice of Jesus saying, " Watch and pray, lest ye enter into temptation." Or we can picture ourselves standing at the foot of the Cross and cast ourselves before Him. Or again we can picture the thoughts that disturb us as the multitude thronging about Jesus, and in spirit call to Him above the noise they make, or force our way through to Him, as in the stories of the Gospel miracles. Our meditations will supply us with similar trains of thought ; if we have the faculty for constructing vivid mental pictures of such incidents it will be all the better. We shall thus substitute a brief and vivid meditation or act of the imagination for the distraction of the moment, and so enable ourselves to elude it ; we can then return to the proper subject of our meditation. Naturally we shall choose such scenes as appeal to us most ; the lives of the Saints may suggest others.

Another method which can sometimes be employed with profit is to use a distracting thought which comes into our minds as a means for raising up our souls to God. For instance, if during our prayers we begin to think of a friend, we can so to speak convert our thought about him into an act of intercession for his particular needs, if known to us, or for his general spiritual welfare. Having thus brought him with us to the throne of grace we can then let him go, while we remain there ourselves. (Obviously the actual wording of this sentence implies a train of pictorial images which we may or may not find helpful.) We can do the same with any good cause in which we are interested, and probably with any of our serious activities we can convert distracting thoughts which arise from them into a prayer that we may perform them to the glory of God. If we were advanced very far in the life of prayer, it is by no means improbable that we should be able to do this even with trivial matters. But most people would probably find it impossible to do so with any reality. If, for instance, our main interest in life is a motor-bicycle, it is hardly likely that the distracting thoughts which such an interest may produce during our prayers will easily be converted into a prayer that we may ride it to the glory of God. If we were sufficiently advanced in holiness we should be able to do so ; we should normally employ any innocent recreation to the glory of God. But as long as we do in fact solely practise it for our own amusement, we shall probably find it impossible to weave such thoughts into the train of our prayers, and we shall have to remedy such distractions by other means. But where the distracting thoughts are concerned with matters which are obviously suitable subjects for intercession, we can rightly convert them into acts of intercessory prayer and then revert to our meditation.

Where our distractions are unusually strong and these methods prove ineffective it may sometimes be necessary to have recourse to reading some book such as a book of the New Testament or the *Imitation of Christ*, or another suitable book of spiritual reading, and to continue reading it on our knees until we either come to a passage which suggests a train of thought capable of occupying our minds, or until the time of our meditation has been completed. Except where our distractions are exceptionally strong, and when there is every reason to suppose that at some later time in the day we shall be able to meditate with greater ease, we should never abandon our prayers merely because of distractions. (The sort of occasion contemplated might arise if we were expecting with anxiety an important piece of news which we could be sure of receiving by the next post.) We must remember that a meditation which seems to us to be made up entirely of a struggle to avoid distractions, and a rather unsuccessful struggle at that, may be of far more value in the sight of God than one which seems to us of great value, but is really nothing but a revel in an access of sensible devotion. The attempt to continue in prayer, when prayer seems worthless and impossible, is an act of Christian virtue ; the other is merely a piece of natural enjoyment. Perseverance in prayer when prayer is difficult may be a very real bearing of the Cross.

Mortification.

A further remedy against distractions is the practice of mortification. A large number of our distractions arise from an undue and unnecessary dissipation of our minds, and we cannot cope with them successfully unless we are prepared to cut off the disease of which they are the symptoms. We must learn to deny ourselves things which the world at any rate regards as harmless, mortifying our natural desires or putting them to death in order that we may substitute for them the love of God. The cares and pleasures and deceitful riches of this world are one of the main causes for the failure of our spiritual development.

The practice of mortification is normally divided into two kinds, voluntary and necessary. By voluntary mortifications are meant any acts of self-discipline which we undertake of our own free-will as a means of growing in holiness ; by necessary are meant those which we cannot omit without falling into sin, or which the circumstances of our daily life make it impossible to avoid. The former class need not be considered here. The voluntary austerities practised by some of the Saints cannot be imitated by those who are only beginners in the spiritual life without presumption ; they should never be undertaken without the advice of someone who is competent to direct us, nor until we have made a considerable amount of progress in the practice of necessary mortification. It may be added that such austerities have usually been undertaken in virtue of a sense of spiritual compulsion or in obedience to superiors and were therefore necessary rather than voluntary.

Consequently in this chapter we shall be concerned only with the practice of necessary mortification. By this is meant the bearing with patience, if not with gladness, the various difficulties and trials which we cannot avoid without sin, or which we cannot avoid in any way at all, whether we would like to or not. The practice of mortification in regard to these trials and annoyances consists in learning to accept these as the will of God, first without grumbling openly, then without inward resentment, and finally with a joyful acceptance of them. Such trials are of many kinds, and it is entirely impossible for anyone to avoid them. They include such things as the tiresome and irritating people among whom we have to live, or whom we are bound to obey, inevitable poverty or ill-health and all the suffering, discomforts and inconveniences of daily life.

In order to avoid a possible misconception it may be well to point out that while the bearing of these things with patience is a necessary Christian duty, this does not mean that the Christian is forbidden to take active steps to remedy them. For instance, it is a duty to bear pain without grumbling at it or making oneself a nuisance to one's neighbours by demanding their sympathy. It is not a duty to bear sickness without going to a doctor for remedy ; it is rather a duty to consult him. It is only when the disease is incurable and the pain cannot be alleviated that patience is the only course open. In the same way it is a duty to bear poverty with patience and resignation ; but except for those who have deliberately chosen a life of poverty for the sake of Christ, it is not necessarily the Christian's duty to accept his poverty without making any attempt to improve his position in the world. It is not the duty of the worker to refuse to strike for higher wages ; but he would, if he were a perfect Christian, do so without ceasing to be in a state of charity towards the employer, however oppressive and tyrannous, against whom he struck. It may be the duty of the Christian to be a rebel ; but ideally he would rebel, even in arms, without malice to the tyrant, whose system of tyranny he felt it his duty to overthrow. It need hardly be added that this is an ideal which only a perfect Saint could attain ; it is the duty of the Christian to endeavour to live up to it as well as he can.

We shall not, however, learn to bear these difficulties with resignation except by the use of prayer. In our meditation we must learn to accept literally the teaching of Our Lord as to the duty of loving our enemies and seeing in the sufferings which we cannot avoid evidence of the love of God. Further in our resolutions it will be a good thing if we frequently look forward to some trial or annoyance which is fairly certain to meet us during the day, and resolve to bear it patiently. Where our prayer consists largely of acts of the will, we ought regularly to include in it acts of resignation, by which we submit our will to the will of God. These acts should not be merely general ; we should once again include among them definite acts of resignation to particular inconveniences or sufferings. These should not merely refer to remote and improbable sufferings of a dramatic and heroic character ; we should not, for instance, paint dramatic pictures of ourselves dying in torment for the sake of preaching the Gospel, when we are not in any way likely to be called upon to do so. It is far more valuable to resign ourselves to an almost inevitable toothache, or an hour in the company of the most tedious of our acquaintances. It may be observed in passing that we are hardly likely to emerge successfully out of the larger trial unless we are capable of enduring the latter.

In this way we shall succeed by degrees in learning to overcome the inevitable dissipation of our minds. We shall learn to see life, not as a multitude of irrelevant and disconnected episodes, but as a system of manifestations of the will of God. Instead of seeing our relation to God as merely one incident among many, confined to the times which we definitely set apart for religion, we shall learn to trace His hand in the whole of life, and so we shall learn in our prayers to refer our distractions to Him as soon as they enter our minds. The thought of a particular person may, for example, come into our minds ; but instead of allowing our minds to wander off into thinking about him, we shall offer automatically an act of intercession for him and so join his needs to the thread of our prayers.   Annoyances of any kind will furnish material for acts of resignation ; we shall even learn to submit with resignation to the temptations which sinful distractions bring, recognizing that our present temptations result from our past sins and are their necessary punishment.

There is further a particular class of distractions which may have to be met by a particular act of mortification.   It will sometimes happen that our distractions are largely concerned with some predominant interest in our lives. That interest may be either sinful or innocent. If it is sinful it is obviously necessary for us to avoid the particular distraction by overcoming the besetting sin from which it arises.   Here we shall have to use the ordinary remedies. It may, however, be an entirely innocent interest, such as our work or our favourite recreation, or a particular friend. In such a case we shall have to use the ordinary remedies against distraction. But it may further be necessary for us to consider whether this particular interest, however innocent in itself, may not be the one thing which is coming between us and God. Very often indeed it will be obvious that we cannot abandon it, as for instance if we find our prayers continually distracted by cares about a family which we are bound to support, or about work which we quite clearly cannot abandon. But it may very often happen that the continual intrusion of such distractions into our prayers is a sign that we are called upon to abandon the cause of them, perhaps as a first instalment of a yet further measure of self-denial. It is not of course to be assumed that, whenever we find any interest of this kind distracting our prayers rather constantly, we ought to abandon it at once. We cannot do without some measure of recreation ; we are not called upon as Christians to give up personal friendships. We should always in the first instance use the ordinary remedies against distractions, and endeavour to refer this particular interest to the will of God. But we should always be prepared for the possibility that the will of God that we should surrender some particular interest, innocent in itself but standing between us and His will for our life, may reveal itself in the first instance by the fact that this interest proves a continual distraction to our prayers. It should be observed that, where after full consideration and the advice of some competent guide we are led to conclude that this is so, the act of mortification which is involved in abandoning this interest is no longer a voluntary but a necessary one.

Further, it must always be remembered that we must be prepared to find that certain pleasures which the world counts innocent may prove as we advance in the practice of prayer to be less innocent than we thought at first, and must therefore be abandoned. There is a good deal in the way of mildly uncharitable gossip and criticism of others or intolerance in our attitude to the beliefs and opinions of others in which the world sees no harm ; yet these things are entirely out of place in the Christian character. There is, on the other hand, much in modern life in which the world sees no harm, but which the serious Christian will, to say the least of it, be well advised to avoid. These failings will provide most of us with abundant material for mortification, especially when we apply them, not only to words and actions, but to our thoughts as well.

VI

THE PRAYER OF SIMPLICITY

Probably, if we persevere long enough in meditation, we shall find it necessary to pass on to the prayer of acts and affections of the will, for the simple reason that we shall find formal reasoning both unprofitable and unnecessary. Further, our acts will gradually develop into "affections" in the sense described above ; that is to say, they will flow more or less easily and spontaneously. This does not mean that there will not be times when we shall find it very hard to resist distractions, or times when we feel hopelessly disinclined for prayer ; but the same difficulty will meet us at the stage of meditation. It may further happen that we shall find our affections losing more and more any specific quality, as of hope, love, contrition or humility. They will, if we reach this stage of development, tend to become more and more a silent communion with God, which includes all these and all other varieties of affections, just because it transcends them. Affections of this type have been described above : the difference is that while they will normally come but rarely into our prayers at the outset, and last only for a very brief period, they will now occupy the main part of our prayers. We may still need a certain amount of formal meditation and forced acts of the will, but these will occupy less and less of our prayers. This kind of prayer is generally described as the "Prayer of Simplicity." We must not be disturbed by supposing that our prayers are too vague to be of any value, nor on the other hand must we mistake this quite normal type of prayer for a high stage of mystical development. All that has happened is that we have learned to fix our souls on God without being forced to remind ourselves continually that we must be doing so : we are loving, instead of forcing ourselves to try to love. For, although in this prayer of simplicity the other attitudes of the soul are present, yet love predominates, and may even leave us no consciousness of the other attitudes. This does not, however, matter, for it is love alone that is the fulfilling of the Law in prayer no less than in life. At the same time, this love is still very imperfect and very far below the conscious love of God felt by the great Saints of the contemplative life ; we are in fact only just beginning to love.

These further stages of prayer do not fall within the scope of this book, which is only intended for beginners. One thing which is certain is that we shall never make any solid advance in the life of prayer unless we are making continual efforts to advance at the same time in the life of imitating the human example of Our Lord. We must be content to know that we shall never succeed ; there will always be fresh heights to climb, but we must be resolved to go forward in whatever direction He may call us. We must never suppose that the life of prayer is a kind of substitute for the life of the service of Jesus. The life of service is impossible without .prayer ; it is equally true that the life of prayer is impossible without service, although that service need not take the form of a life of active good works in the obvious sense. We must never hope that any true life of prayer is compatible with an easy-going and comfortable Christianity ; there is no way of evading Our Lord's warning, " If any man will serve Me, let him deny himself and take up his cross and follow Me."